D0464576

PRAISE FOR
COMPETING WITH GIANTS

A generous sharing of business methods and experiences. Of benefit to everyone, from entrepreneurs and start-ups to multinationals focused on improving their success in emerging markets and understanding the changing face of globalization.

WILLIAM M. DOHENY

CEO, Oceans International

Former General Manager, Coca-Cola Vietnam

A great story about drive, persistence, and risk taking. Dr. Thanh's journey from an orphanage to founding and leading Vietnam's largest beverage company should be an inspiration to entrepreneurs everywhere. This book is an important illustration of why companies must keep innovating to stay ahead in a hyper-competitive environment.

KEITH HARRISON

Former Head of Global Product Supply, P&G

An insightful look into what it takes to go from good to great in an emerging Asian economy and as a family-owned business. As a former pugilist, Dr. Thanh not only has a keen sense for the art and skill of boxing but also the art and skill of business strategy.

ANDREW MACDONALD

Corporate Senior Vice President and CCO, Marina Bay Sands

It's rare to see a local brand rise to such heights and compete on the same level as the MNCs. Its example will inspire and motivate homegrown industries to realize their dreams, muster their confidence, and truly compete with giants.

WAI PHYO

Managing Director, Yathar Cho Industry Ltd.

An unmissable insight into how and why Vietnamese businesses are quietly growing into global players. A must read.

HIROSHI OTSUKA

President and CEO, Musashi Seimitsu

[This book] shines a light on a fascinating family whose "nothing is impossible" attitude and entrepreneurial spirit has fashioned such a successful company. A microscopic investigation of the dynamism driving companies across Asia.

VU N. DUONG

Professor, Nanyang Technological University

Great insights into how to combine local knowledge with international best practices to create brands that can compete on a global level. An amazing story about the growth of a Vietnamese company.

CK MOHAN

Former Senior HR Director, Yum Restaurants International

COMPETING WITH GIANTS

How One Family-Owned Company Took On
the Multinationals and Won

Competing
with
Giants

PHƯƠNG UYÊN TRẦN

WITH JACKIE HORNE AND JOHN KADOR

FOREWORD BY BRIAN TRACY

ForbesBooks

Published by ForbesBooks, Charleston, South Carolina.
Member of Advantage Media Group.

ForbesBooks is a registered trademark, and the ForbesBooks colophon is a trademark of Forbes Media, LLC.

Printed in the United States of America.

10 9 8 7 6 5 4 3 2 1

ISBN: 978-1-946633-15-6
LCCN: 2018942091

Cover design by Carly Blake.
Layout design by Megan Elger.

This publication is designed to provide accurate and authoritative information in regard to the subject matter covered. It is sold with the understanding that the publisher is not engaged in rendering legal, accounting, or other professional services. If legal advice or other expert assistance is required, the services of a competent professional person should be sought.

Advantage Media Group is proud to be a part of the Tree Neutral® program. Tree Neutral offsets the number of trees consumed in the production and printing of this book by taking proactive steps such as planting trees in direct proportion to the number of trees used to print books. To learn more about Tree Neutral, please visit **www.treeneutral.com**.

Since 1917, the Forbes mission has remained constant. Global Champions of Entrepreneurial Capitalism. ForbesBooks exists to further that aim by bringing the Stories, Passion, and Knowledge of top thought leaders to the forefront. ForbesBooks brings you The Best in Business. To be considered for publication, please visit **www.forbesbooks.com**.

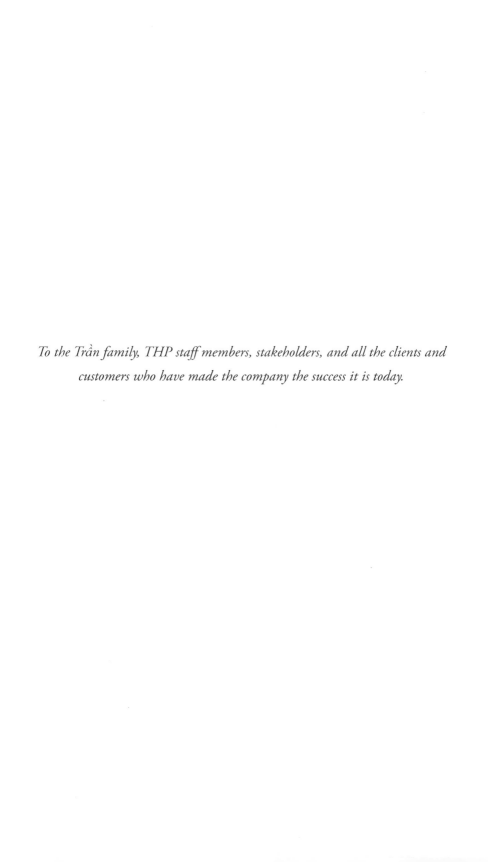

To the Trần family, THP staff members, stakeholders, and all the clients and customers who have made the company the success it is today.

TABLE OF CONTENTS

FOREWORD

VIETNAM! What images its name evokes in the minds of my generation and so many millions of Americans. Few other countries have exerted such a hold over our collective imagination.

It's been half a century since I first went to Asia in 1968. That year was one of the bloodiest of the Vietnam War and I spent two years in the country calling customers and selling international investments to Vietnamese and American businessmen. I witnessed incredible suffering, but also the immense fortitude and determination of the Vietnamese people.

Those traits are what I see on display now when I visit the country for my speaking tours and seminars, for I was lucky enough to go back again for the first time in 2012.

How much had changed by then. After the war, Vietnam began experiencing the fastest wealth creation in its history, and that growth still continues today.

The transformation is astounding. Vietnam's industrious, entrepreneurial nature is creating bustling cities and a dynamic economy.

The country is repeating a pattern we have already seen across East Asia as Japan, and later South Korea, Taiwan, and China, rose from the ashes of World War II to global prominence.

We are all aware that the world's attention is pivoting toward Asia. This is what makes this book so important.

It is time to see Vietnam the way its people see it—forward looking, keen to learn, and eager to grow. Each time I return to the country, I am struck by the enthusiasm of its young population.

It is also important to understand how much they have to offer us. Human values are universal, but history and culture can shape those values in different ways. The West and the East can learn and benefit from each other.

So when a book like *Competing with Giants* comes along, I really pay attention. This is a story that resonates on so many levels.

On the one hand, it shows how Dr. Thanh and his wife, Madam Nu, overcame all manner of hardships after the war to turn THP into one of Vietnam's most prominent and fast-moving consumer goods companies. At the same time, it provides many valuable insights about how Asian companies and their founders think and behave, which we can all learn from.

I have spent my entire working life helping people muster internal resources, overcome obstacles, and find their way to success and achievement. In this book, we have two clear examples of this in practice on both the corporate and personal level.

THP is a family-run business led by Dr. Thanh. Today he has his daughters, Phương and Bích, by his side. Their example shows what women are also now able to achieve.

The whole family lives by the motto that "nothing is impossible." They dream big, take action each day to achieve their goals, and never give up.

Their company's history demonstrates all these traits in action. It reveals a bigger truth about how small businesses can effectively compete with corporate "giants" if their owners are prepared to set goals, take chances, and learn from their successes and failures.

There are also important lessons about how to manage that growth by developing a set of core values. These help companies to achieve and refine their goals by embedding them into every employee who walks through the door. For what is success unless you can help others to learn from it?

In one sense, THP has been lucky because it has been able to take advantage of Vietnam's fast growth. But as I say in so many of my books, luck is predictable. If you take more chances, you will find more opportunities wherever you are in life.

I wish I had known of Dr. Thanh and his remarkable family when I wrote *The 21 Success Secrets of Self-Made Millionaires*. I'm sure their story would have illuminated the set of principles or "universal laws," which are the foundations of successful business people everywhere.

Competing with Giants demonstrates how Dr. Thanh, like all self-made millionaires, practices these twenty-one success secrets. One very important secret concerns money. The goal is not to achieve it but to become the kind of person who earns it and then holds onto it.

Dr. Thanh also demonstrates the power of staying focused and positive despite hardship and setbacks. Like all successful people, he has learned to take responsibility for his actions and emotions.

Negative emotions will cause your brain to shut down, resulting in poor judgment and bad decision-making. The lesson is clear: remain positive and levelheaded.

Anyone interested in succeeding against adversity and improving their competitive advantage should carefully study this book. By realizing the market value of leadership and clarity of vision, readers will be able to understand that obstacles—even those that appear to be giants—can be managed on the path to success.

Brian Tracy
San Diego, California
May 2018

$2.5 BILLION.

That is the amount of money we walked away from in 2012. This was the figure The Coca-Cola Company had offered to acquire a controlling interest in Tân Hiệp Phát Beverage Group (THP), the family-owned business my parents founded in 1994.

As I sat in that glass-encased conference room at Coca-Cola's headquarters, my head was spinning. I glanced nervously at my father, my heart beating furiously. With only that glance, I knew why he had been so successful. His drive, determination, and self-belief were etched all over his sixty years. His poker face fixed, his eyes focused, and his face hewn from his boxing days. He gave nothing away.

Coca-Cola had dispatched a private jet for us, flying us from New York to Atlanta for a private audience with the then-CEO, Muhtar Kent. Everyone knew why we were there: Coca-Cola was interested in acquiring THP. These negotiations would decide the terms.

Coca-Cola wanted us to share their dream. Their presentations were designed to impress us, overawe us even. Most people would have been bowled over.

Sitting across the negotiating table from us were executives from one of the world's biggest multinational corporations (MNC). According to *Forbes's* rankings, Coca-Cola also owns the fifth most recognizable brand after Apple, Google, Microsoft, and Facebook.

It is a giant in every sense of the word. In 2012, it generated revenues of $48 billion, and there was no corner of the planet where it was not aggressively marketing its products, including Vietnam. In fact, Kent had visited the country earlier in the year and pledged to invest an additional $300 million over the next three.

Both sides were aware of Vietnam's potential as its citizens' incomes and spending power rose. Never was this clearer than when we visited Mexico at Coca-Cola's invitation. The country ranks as Coke's number one global market, accounting for about 11 percent of sales back in 2012. At that time, the average Mexican consumer was buying almost 160 liters of soft drinks per annum, compared to just below 30 liters in Vietnam.

Yet as we negotiated back and forth in Atlanta, it was obvious there was a Vietnamese-sized elephant in the room. Coca-Cola showed us their plans to grab ever more market share across the emerging markets. But if we agreed to their terms, THP would only be allowed to expand its own market share in Vietnam, Laos, and Cambodia.

We would have to hand over our export business to Thailand, Australia, and other parts of Asia. The terms specifically restricted THP from venturing into markets outside those three countries.

The agreement also required THP to give up new product development. This constraint would have undercut one of our core strengths: THP's record of product innovation achieved from a hard-won understanding of the Vietnamese market and its consumers. It had generated our bestselling products, including Dr. Thanh Herbal Tea, Zero Degree Green Tea, Number 1 Energy Drink, Number 1 Soya Milk, Number 1 Active, and Number 1 Juicie Fruit.

The provisions were nothing less than a deal breaker for us. THP's vision was, and still is, to expand throughout Asia and beyond with new and exciting brands. We rejected Coca-Cola's offer, walking away from the $2.5 billion payday and the history books. If the deal had gone ahead, it would have been the largest-ever foreign acquisition in Vietnam's history by deal value. It still would be the second largest today.

It was not what the Coca-Cola executives had been expecting at all. As the elevator doors closed on their surprised faces, my father moved his hand to mine, gently smiled, and whispered like the gambler he has always been.

"Never show emotion; never show your hand," he said. "Proud we stand, as we always have and as we always will. A partnership should be exactly that, a meeting of minds tied together by a shared passion. What we just experienced was not a meeting of minds."

I have never felt so proud or strong-willed as the elevator whisked us down to the lobby. For it is never easy to compete with giants, let alone face them down.

Squaring off against a much bigger competitor requires nerves of steel, particularly one that hails from the richest and most powerful country on the planet. But my father taught me a valuable lesson that day: understand our values and what our company stands for, what direction we are heading in, and above all else, do not be dazzled by the power that multinational companies are able to display.

After returning from Atlanta we explored other arrangements with Coca-Cola, but nothing came of it. Our visions were just too different. So, we walked away from the $2.5 billion and said thanks, but no thanks.

My father taught me a valuable lesson that day: understand our values and what our company stands for, what direction we are heading in, and above all else, do not be dazzled by the power that multinational companies are able to display.

Perhaps one day THP and Coca-Cola could be partners, but at that point in time, we remained competitors. In the ensuing years, THP has attracted attention from other global brands, including PepsiCo, plus the Japanese companies Ito En and Asahi.

We are David to their Goliath in terms of revenues and operating history. However, that does not mean we had a weak negotiating hand when we were dealing with Coca-Cola—far from it. We had been successfully competing against them for almost twenty years. We were outselling both Coke and Pepsi in non-carbonated alternatives such as teas and energy drinks.

One of the reasons for this success was THP's product line of healthier alternatives compared to the vast melee of sugary soft drinks, which had made Coca-Cola one of the world's most successful companies. Ours was a market segment that Coca-Cola was keen to move into, so we had been on the alert for any predatory approaches.

But how had one local Vietnamese company carved out that market share for itself in the first place and from nothing? Play word association with most foreigners and the words that still most usually spring to their minds about Vietnam relate to the war, to the boat people, or perhaps to a nice holiday in the sun. They generally do not involve a dynamic, fast-moving consumer-goods company with global ambitions.

This book hopes to rectify that, to explain how it is possible to build a thriving local company and turn it into a national champion. At its heart, it is about how two very determined individuals emerged from the ashes of the Vietnam War and fought their way through numerous hardships to create a company that produces some of Vietnam's best-loved drinks brands.

How they learned to adopt the best international standards while navigating the challenges of domestic upheaval and US sanctions. How they resisted the moneyed courting of multinationals like Coca-Cola and became stronger as a result. How they successfully rode the wave of Vietnam's growth, as the country arises from devastation and chaos to take its place alongside Asia's most vibrant economies.

Today THP is still independent, but that does not mean the company is not open to partnerships with multinationals or other companies. We *are*—as long as they are win-win partnerships. What this book aims to show is that local companies can easily stand their ground against the multinationals and prosper. Local companies have many advantages, some of which they may not even be fully aware of.

Globalization, which propels the multinationals, can seem like a powerful, almost irresistible force. This is particularly the case across the emerging and frontier markets where many independent companies like THP may have only recently become national leaders, wondering how they can fend off these global giants who have suddenly become interested in their country.

We hope THP's example will inspire other companies that hope to follow suit but may lack the confidence to face the giants head-on.

It is always good to remember that today's global giants were once small companies trying to find their own way, too.

The landscape around them can change very quickly. Asia is rising, and this means the Western-style multinationals are being forced to come up with new strategies. Part I of this book describes how the region's growing clout is reshaping the way they operate. It will examine the different approaches multinationals and local companies take, exploring the advantages and disadvantages of each.

Chapter 1 analyzes why there has been such a long-held assumption that globalization is the best pathway to prosperity and a more cooperative, peaceful world. Few doubt that globalization has created the foundations for success and helped expand global trade. It has helped forge the multinationals as we know them.

Yet people in both developed and developing countries are increasingly challenging whether it is the only path to success. Across the developed world, a rising call for protectionism has triggered some surprising results in the geopolitical arena—the shock of the Brexit vote and the result of the US 2016 election being two standout examples.

For Vietnam and some of our Asian neighbors, the big globalization hope rested on the twelve-country-strong Trans-Pacific Partnership (TPP). That dream suffered a setback following the US withdrawal in January 2017. But talks continued to move ahead and, in March 2018, the new Comprehensive and Progressive Agreement for Trans-Pacific Partnership was signed by eleven countries, not including the US. One month later, US President Donald Trump said he would like America to join if it could get a "better" deal.

As Asia's power rises on the world stage, its governments are increasingly questioning whether it is a good idea to give multinationals a free ride. Why let them come charging into a country and buy up its crown jewels? Why become part of someone else's global supply chain?

Instead, many Asian governments are actively seeking to foster domestic champions of their own. Some of these champions have already reached a large enough size to expand overseas and forge partnerships with other companies in the region. We may be witnessing the birth of a new type of multinational: the Asian multinational.

Vietnam has also reached an economic juncture where its biggest companies, like THP, are starting to create a regional footprint in addition to riding rapidly rising domestic GDP at home. Chapter 2 explores why Vietnam has become such an attractive and compelling proposition for multinationals and how domestic companies, particularly in the private sector, have been more than a match for them.

> *We may be witnessing the birth of a new type of multinational: the Asian multinational.*

Chapter 3 will take a more in-depth look at how Vietnam's history forged my parents' identities and how the two combined to make THP the company it is today, for THP's success cannot be taken out of the context of what is happening in Vietnam. Likewise, it is not possible to understand THP without that same knowledge about my parents who share many of the same personality traits as successful entrepreneurs all over the world.

But even so, successful local companies like THP do not just materialize from nowhere. They must be created and, more importantly, they must be sustained under the onslaught of both local and foreign competition.

Part II identifies the key principles that all companies need to take into consideration if they want to succeed. It also looks at how Asian values shape the region's businesses and what all companies can learn from East and West to enhance their operations and customer reach.

Each chapter takes a different principle and demonstrates how THP has applied it. These are: Create Authentic Local Products (chapter 4); Adhere to International Standards (chapter 5); Govern Growth (chapter 6); Motivate Employees and Foster Community Spirit (chapter 7) and Take Responsibility (chapter 8).

Part III of the book discusses the role of women in Asian business. In chapter 9, I share my personal story, which I am pleased to report is increasingly representative of women from emerging nations who work hard to educate themselves and thirst to take on leadership roles. I am someone who was born and lives in Vietnam but was educated abroad. I believe my own life story demonstrates that it is possible to have a global and a local mind-set to the benefit of both.

Chapter 10 discusses how the role of women is changing in Vietnam through the lives of my grandmother, my mother, and now my sister Bích and myself. Ours is still a male-dominated society, but women are starting to make their mark and THP is working hard to make sure that women have an equal voice.

This book discusses many challenges and lessons, but the overall message is a positive one. A simple glance at the headlines can be depressing. But there is little to be gained from stewing in the doom and gloom sensationalized by the media. It is always good to remember that one person's threat is another person's opportunity.

There is little doubt we are living in a fast-evolving period of social change, and sometimes it might appear we are powerless to resist the tide of globalization. However, there is also evidence that we still live in a world on an upward trajectory, as more and more people interconnect via a growing network tied together by the knowledge economy.

The world I have been fortunate to grow up in is dramatically different from the war-torn world my parents experienced. The world the next generation inherits will be different than anything I have experienced. There is only one thing we can all be sure of: the world will be what we collectively make it. And that is why I am so excited about the book you hold in your hands and the journey we are embarking on together.

Phương Uyên Trần
Ho Chi Minh City, Vietnam
May 2018

Part I:
Asia Rising

Asia is shaping a new world order. For many centuries, European countries and more recently their North American cousins dominated global trade, often colonizing many of the countries they operated in. They gave birth to the multinational companies and a new age of economic imperialism through corporate globalization.

That is now changing. Asian economies are growing rapidly and so is the wealth of their nations' citizens. It is now Asian companies that are expanding across the globe.

Will they bring a new set of corporate values with them? Asians believe in yin and yang. We value balance and harmony. There is no reason why these principles cannot be applied to the corporate sector, too.

Localism and globalization can co-exist and feed off each other in positive ways. So, too, can small domestic companies across emerging as well as developed economies also enjoy significant strengths and advantages over the seemingly all-powerful multinationals.

This section of the book explores how Asia's increasing economic power is changing the rules of the game and how Vietnam and companies like THP are learning to play by them.

CHAPTER 1

The World Reaches
Peak Multinational

PLACE MATTERS. Yet that message has become increasingly lost on many of the world's multinationals, even though their promotional literature will tell you otherwise. The Holy Grail of marketing is supposed to be the Four Ps: place, price, product, and promotion.

However, big global corporations frequently fail to understand the cultural nuances of the new countries they are targeting with their products. Increasingly, many of these big companies have also become politically and economically detached from their home countries as well.

> *Big global corporations frequently fail to understand the cultural nuances of the new countries they are targeting with their products.*

They are literally everywhere, but they no longer seem to belong to anywhere. One of the biggest challenges facing the world is how countries can find the tools to manage and reign in these global behemoths when their governments know they are in competition for their resources with other countries keen to attract their business.

It was all very different back in the mid-1970s when those last helicopters were lifting people out of the American embassy in Saigon. Multinationals were not the force they are today. In 1975, international trade flows were still very small, with world exports amounting to just 16.3 percent of the world's combined GDP. But the engine of global trade was starting to whir. Fast-forward to 2008 and that figure had almost doubled to peak at 30.7 percent of global GDP.

In the intervening four decades, a number of trends helped multinationals to colonize the world as the governments of the high-income countries they originated from did before them. Firstly, a revolution in digital communications facilitated cheaper long-distance telephone calls, followed by faxed documents, and finally the Internet age. Communication barriers collapsed.

Secondly, from the 1980s onward, new ways of economic thinking promoted the benefits of unfettered capitalism over organized labor. The Reagan and Thatcher administrations in the US and UK believed that "greed is good" and promoted privatization and less government. As Socialist governments crumbled across Eastern Europe, it appeared the West reigned supreme—or the world had reached "the end of history" as Francis Fukuyama so famously put it.

During the 1990s, big new markets were opening up all over the world. The East Asian tigers were roaring. China began to industrialize rapidly, while India shook off the License Raj (its unwieldy bureaucracy) and the European Union became an ever-bigger trading bloc as it embraced its Eastern European cousins. Investment and trade flows accelerated. Cross-border M&A (mergers and acquisitions) were frenetic.

Multinationals became richer and bigger as they extended their tentacles into ever-more countries. The companies in their supply chains followed suit. It was supposed to be a win-win situation.

Developing countries would benefit because their populations would be lifted out of poverty from backbreaking agricultural work into shiny new factories and offices. In many cases, that was true. Vietnam has been a huge beneficiary of that trend since the turn of the century.

Developed countries were also supposed to benefit as multinationals' soaring stock prices underwrote workers' pension and insurance plans. However, the global financial crisis of 2007 was a major watershed, which blew many long-held notions apart.

In many ways, 2007 was the apex of globalization. World exports have never hit that peak again, although they did re-bound back to 30.5 percent in 2011 before starting to fall again. The World Bank's most recent figure for 2016 had them at 28.575 percent.

Since the global financial crisis, we have been experiencing an ever-greater backlash against globalization and the stirrings of protectionism, although this has not stopped multinationals from continuing to expand across developing markets. There has been a re-think, which is particularly evident in developed markets, where many people no longer believe a borderless corporate world makes sense.

Politically, Brexit and Trump are manifestations of deep anger among working class and increasingly middle-class citizens who feel their jobs and children's futures are being hollowed out. It started with blue-collar workers in the 1980s and, increasingly, white-collar citizens are watching with anger and dismay as their accounting, IT, and legal work is outsourced to cheaper countries.

Multinationals, meanwhile, have generated far higher profits, but their home countries and populations do not feel they are benefitting from that wealth anymore. Britain's *Guardian* newspaper recently estimated that multinationals are shifting about $745 billion to tax havens each year. That money may be boosting their bottom line, but many believe those profits are only being paid out to a tiny elite.

People often quote the figures produced by the US Economic Policy Institute. These show that US CEOs were paid 20.1 times more than their average worker in 1965. By 1989, that figure had more than doubled to 59.1 times. But the real widening happened over the next three decades as globalization really sped up. In 2016, it stood at 276 times. Unless it is checked, this kind of inequality will threaten the fabric of any society.

And then there is the question of whether those executives deserve it. Operationally, many of these multinationals have failed to generate returns that come anywhere close to matching the growth of C-suite compensation. This disparity is because multinationals' size often works against them. By contrast, remaining locals can have significant advantages particularly during the early years as a company scales up.

Multinationals: Less Flexible, Less Accountable

Cross-border trade, migration of talent, and capital investment all require centralized control and detachment of accountability. Decision-makers operate thousands of miles from where the impacts of those decisions are felt.

Accountability is severed and that can have severe consequences. Multinationals are the corporate version of political entities like the Roman Empire and Han Dynasty. Once they get to a certain size, empires start fraying at the edges and inevitably experience overreach and collapse.

Many multinationals struggle to establish operational procedures that keep far-flung offshoots in line with central policy without stifling their ability to conduct good business. One very good example of this issue in action has been the experience of global banks in the years following the global financial crisis. Many ended up being fined after admitting that local branches had been processing drug-trafficking proceeds and funds from sanctioned countries.

When a multinational gets too big, one solution is for the center to impose more control. However, this can prove counter-productive, adding layers of rigid bureaucracy, which slows down the decision-making process and suffocates employees in red tape. Smaller, more independent companies often move much quicker than multinationals.

THP, for example, has streamlined planning processes and execution abilities. We are far nimbler. One clear benefit comes when we want to invest in new technology. We can invest in it further down the line than multinationals.

Often that means THP can invest in technology that is more developed than what multinationals are using. And even when the same technology is deployed, THP can often exploit the latest versions of it faster and more productively.

My father says local companies can perform a kind of jujitsu, using the apparent advantages of the multinationals against them.

For example, it is true that multinationals can throw more resources at any given situation than a local company.

But those resources are often thrown blindly, creating problems and wasting time. Local companies, being relatively poor, learn to be smarter and faster.

"We have to aim well," my father says. "One bullet had better hit two targets."

> *Local companies, being relatively poor, learn to be smarter and faster. "We have to aim well," my father says. "One bullet had better hit two targets."*

Even when multinationals are smart about the resources they deploy, they are still slow because of the bureaucratic layers and multiple time zones. By contrast, THP is a family-owned business led by its founder. This means THP can execute a business decision about any issue before a multinational has probably even convened a staff meeting to discuss it.

My father often makes tough decisions like this: "When an issue comes up, I'll listen to my team and then sleep on the decision," he says. "I'll announce my decision the next day or the day after. Sometimes I'll get it right. Sometimes I'll get it wrong. Either way we'll know the answer quickly. In the long run, our ability to make quick decisions, even faulty ones, outweighs the advantages of excessive deliberation."

In addition, multinationals' sheer size often makes them wary about introducing new products because they fear success may come at the expense of existing products. Fear of cannibalization is often why market leaders are slow to adopt change.

In the case of Vietnam's consumer-beverage market, Coca-Cola offers Coke drinks and a number of other carbonated soft drinks.

THP offers green-tea drinks, a category we believe Coca-Cola delayed introducing for fear of taking sales away from its leading products.

Multinationals will never care as much as a local owner does. We literally have skin in the game. As my father notes, "My accountability is extreme and unavoidable. That focuses my attention in a way that multinational executives can't be expected to share."

When THP develops a new beverage, the very first people who drink it are family members. So, the incentives to develop products of the highest-possible quality are intense. What multinational can match that level of commitment?

For a family concern, their very economic survival is at stake. For a multinational, it typically represents another skirmish whose outcome is but a rounding error in the annual report.

The people who lead multinationals are professional and determined, but they allocate resources in proportion to a market's revenue opportunities and often no more. Family-owned businesses dedicate 100 percent of their resources to protect their investment and legacy.

Local Companies: Society's Foundation

The multinational approach has its disadvantages, but this does not mean that globalization is a bad thing. Opening up trade borders tends to open up minds as well, and that is a good thing. I personally see myself as both a citizen of Vietnam and a global citizen. I do not believe these two identities are in conflict. Both identities give meaning to my life and help me fulfill THP's mission as a major player in the global FMCG (fast moving consumer goods) sector.

But globalization needs a different slant. Perhaps its benefits are best realized when participants stay genuinely grounded in the local economies they operate in. For me, a local business means an independent buisness and often a family-owned one. These businesses try to honor the needs and interests of all stakeholders at the same time as building long-term profitability.

Communities are healthier and more sustainable if they are supported by local businesses, which have a tangible stake in their success. It creates a virtuous circle, resulting in higher living standards and greater personal accountability for the long-term wellbeing of our communities and the environment we all have a stake in.

Multinationals often claim they are committed to building prosperity right where people live, and they make a big point of aiming their Corporate Social Responsibility (CSR) budgets locally. But the reality is often very different from the rhetoric.

Consumers are starting to see through this. The relationships and associations they tend to value most are local—although when countries enter the first stage of rapid industrialization that can get lost for a while.

There is generally a stage in a country's early development when consumers are overawed by foreign brands. They want to display their new wealth by demonstrating they have the ability to buy expensive foreign goods. It sets them apart from other citizens who have not yet reached that income level.

China was a great example of this during the first decade of the twenty-first century with its lines of eager shoppers hoping to buy the latest Gucci handbag or Apple iPhone. But China started to enter a new stage of development around the mid-2010s. This was the point when homegrown companies had moved far enough up the value chain to produce well-known brands of their own. As a result, Chinese customers have started trusting their own brands and have become clearly proud of them. They are just as likely to buy a Huawei smartphone as an Apple one.

Vietnam has followed a similar route but a couple of decades later than China because of the war, which stymied the country's development. However, as will become clear throughout this book, Vietnam is a country with a geographical divide. Northerners are far more likely to be transfixed by foreign brands than Southerners. They are far more status-conscious and rely on referrals.

Statistics also show that while people embrace the benefits of globalization, they also want to preserve their identities and traditions. The world may be flatter, but that does not mean globalization is making everyone the same. Local traditions are becoming more important, not less.

This paradox often demonstrates itself in a preference for buying local brands, particularly in the fresh-food category. This is certainly not that surprising on health grounds. Consumer preference for locally sourced produce holds true for nearly every fresh-food category and is most clearly expressed in highly perishable food categories such as seafood, dairy products, and fruit juices.

In Western countries, the wheel really has come full circle. In the 1960s and 1970s, many consumers abandoned local markets and independent traders to shop in supermarkets where there was a lot more choice and everything had fancy packaging. At the higher-income bracket, that trend is now reversing. Consumers are flocking to re-branded "farmers' markets."

They patronize them because they believe the products are fresher and they are helping the environment by buying products grown locally. But there is also a financial motivation. Consumers want their money to end up in local farmers' pockets and not those of the supermarket giants they believe are trying to wring every last ounce of profit from their supply chains.

THP understands this, and commitment to the community is one of our seven core values (see appendix 2, page 188). Throughout this book, you will hear a lot of mention of the company's core values. The whole company is built around them, and posters of these values are prominently displayed in every work area.

We strive to ensure our employees live and breathe them every day. Each employee can cite the THP values by heart. These values are often woven into the songs they compose and sing when we celebrate the company's anniversary each year. They are the kind of measures that enable companies to develop cohesive corporate cultures.

From Start-Ups to the Sharing Economy

This trend toward localism is manifesting itself in several other ways. Governments are conscious that new job growth flows from entrepreneurial activity usually channeled through start-ups. The smart ones do not try to pick winners and losers, but create the infrastructure and encourage the investment formation which facilitates them.

This kind of entrepreneurial activity has many benefits. It unlocks an individual's power to grow business ideas into successful companies, creating new jobs in the process. It promotes collaboration between business sectors, investors, civil society, universities, and philanthropists to the benefit of society as a whole. Global investors recognize start-ups as an efficient place to park their capital.

Successful start-ups create ripples of economic value up and down the supply chain. Many are now founded on the principle of sharing economy, which is frequently global in scope but local in terms of where the profits end up. The disrupters—the Ubers, eBays and Airbnbs of this world—share some multinational-like characteristics. But they have not had the same free ride across the developing world that earlier multinationals had before them.

The sharing economy is a recent phenomenon; and as a result, emerging and developed markets started fostering these kinds of companies on an almost equal footing. This partly explains why, for example, China's homegrown ride-hailing start-ups like Didi Chuxing have been able to drive Uber out of the country.

We have all gotten used to reading headlines about the breakdown of trust in institutions. But the rise of the sharing economy and peer-to-peer marketplaces like Lending Club demonstrate a move toward cooperative relationships and more collaborative forms of consumption. Companies such as Uber and Airbnb are creating new forms of communities.

All these marketplaces rely on reputation, trust, and reciprocity to thrive. This type of trust-building is called social proof. The eBay marketplace is a great example of it in action: millions of people who do not know each other feel comfortable enough to engage in transactions of trust. It is easier to trust someone when there is ample evidence that hundreds or thousands of other people in the community trust that individual, too.

Multinationals Have Their Benefits

Companies that become too big or dominant tend to attract criticism. But multinationals are still thriving for a reason. They have much to teach because they have learned so much from all the different countries they operate in.

There are many areas where consumers value them highly. Global brands have a clear advantage in some categories. For example, in most developing regions, consumers prefer global brands for baby food and baby formula.

This desire is particularly strong in China, thanks to highly publicized stories about adulterated local products. Consumers there believe that baby products from highly regulated economies in Europe and North America carry an extra quality assurance for which they are willing to pay a premium.

Vietnam has taken this one step further. As chapter 2 will explain, the country has a love/hate relationship with China. Many Vietnamese do not trust Chinese products and tend to shun them because of all the food scandals.

When multinationals enter a market, they almost always raise quality and service standards as well. Local companies should try to emulate this, especially when it comes to corporate governance, as chapters 5 and 6 will explain. Consumers also enjoy the lower prices that accompany a multinational's market entrance, although many do not realize lower prices are frequently a temporary benefit.

This is exactly what happened when Coke and Pepsi entered Vietnam in the 1990s. They got lucky because the state-owned companies were inefficient, and the private sector was still small and weak.

Within a decade, they had easily seen off state-owned Tribeco and Chương Dương from the private sector. By 2000, they felt secure enough to start hiking prices. Once a multinational has successfully eliminated the local competition, prices inevitably go up.

To keep up, local companies must invest and create products and services that are, in every way, equal or better than what the multinationals are offering. Chapter 4 will explore this dynamic in more detail. Neither Tribeco nor Chương Dương mounted an adequate response, and they paid the price. The imperative to improve not only applies to the actual product and its branding but also the sourcing, logistics, and supply chain: everything that helps foster customer satisfaction.

The Costs of Independence

Local companies must adopt world-class standards and marry them with their local knowledge to beat multinationals at their own game. But once a successful local company has national scale, it frequently becomes an acquisition target for multinationals. Companies committed to independence often face offers of cooperation from richer and stronger corporate partners. And there is a cost to turning them down.

The most obvious immediate cost is the loss of financial riches from selling all or part of a company. But there is a bigger and more dangerous long-term cost as well. If a stronger partner cannot create a deal with a local partner like THP, it will often decide to become a more aggressive competitor instead. This is what happened when THP turned down Coca-Cola's offer in 2012.

Some years earlier, Coca-Cola started increasing its marketing budget to create more development opportunities and win more market share in Vietnam's growing beverage sector. THP monitored these investments as we do with any competitor. Coca-Cola's Vietnamese operations expanded. Soon it was promoting products such as Fanta, Sprite, Joy bottled water, Minute Maid fruit juice, and Dasani mineral water.

But it also wanted to grab market share by serving Vietnam's growing young population who were buying healthier and less carbonated beverages. In June 2014, Coca-Cola put four new bottling plants into production in Ho Chi Minh City and Hanoi. By 2015 it had invested up to $500 million in Vietnam.

Meeting of brands but not minds: Tran family with former Coca-Cola CEO, Muhtar Kent, discussing the sale of a controlling stake in THP (2012)

It was from this position of power that Coca-Cola approached THP for partnership discussions. Nevertheless, THP maintained its independence and, despite increased competition, its market share, also.

The decision to keep THP independent was consistent with our understanding of the market. My father is a man of many mottos. His key one is that we exist to serve the customer at a profit. If THP can consistently focus on this central goal, we will control the market. But no one ever said it would be easy.

CHAPTER 2

The Vietnamese Tiger
Starts to Roar

GLOBALIZATION HAS ITS LIMITATIONS, but there is no doubt it has propelled Vietnam to where it is today. Hanoi, Ho Chi Minh (or Saigon as the locals call it), and Danang are cities thick with development. I live in Saigon, which is blooming into a world-class city. Its streets are lined with shops selling expensive luxury goods and its roads are bustling with motorcycles and the latest automobile brands.

One of the reasons you may be reading this book is to understand Vietnam's great potential, which is unfolding before my eyes. Vietnam has reached that crucial stage of development when a country makes its once-in-a-lifetime transition from poverty to prosperity.

Many foreign companies and investors want to tap into that and profit from it. But there is no reason why the Vietnamese cannot drive their own destiny. Vietnamese companies, large and small, are the ones best placed to understand and fulfill their fellow citizens'

> *There is no reason why the Vietnamese cannot drive their own destiny. Vietnamese companies, large and small, are the ones best placed to understand and fulfill their fellow citizens' needs. We hope THP's example encourages others to believe they can do it, too.*

needs. We hope THP's example encourages others to believe they can do it, too.

The simple fact is that as Vietnam gets richer, it becomes an ever-enticing proposition for multinationals hoping to sell their goods. In addition to this, average wages are still low enough to make Vietnam an attractive place for them to set up their factories as well.

The country has become a manufacturing hot spot at the expense of neighboring China where labor costs are much higher. Many companies also feel Vietnam is a stable place to base their operations for the long-term.

It is a potent mix, made all the headier, because in Vietnam, many see echoes of the East Asia tigers: traditionally Hong Kong, Singapore, South Korea, and Taiwan, which made that developmental leap in the 1960s and 1970s. More recently, people look at how China has transformed itself—and many believe Vietnam is next.

Throughout the past fifty years other countries have tried to make that leap but have ended up mired in the middle-income trap, or stifled by corruption. Vietnam will be successful because it shares many of the same traits as the East Asians. What we share are ethnically homogenous societies underpinned by varying degrees of

Confucian ethics, which prioritize respect for elders, harmony (yin and yang), education, and politeness.

The Vietnamese also share East Asia's extremely strong work ethic and entrepreneurial streak. But the country's recent history sets it apart—one that ironically makes foreign companies feel far more comfortable in Vietnam today than in many other Asian countries.

Vietnam is a geopolitical linchpin between the Far East and Southeast Asia. As a result, the country has long been coveted by others and spent a good deal of its history fending off incursions. But it also means it has interacted with many nations and is used to dealing with them.

In some instances that history has left a physical imprint, which today's foreigners can readily identify with. For example, Western-ers tend to like Vietnam because they feel right at home among the colonial buildings instituted by the French—and we serve good coffee. (As a matter of fact, many believe Vietnam serves the world's *best* coffee.)

But it is important to understand how the Vietnamese view this legacy; we no longer see either these buildings or drinks as French—but rather as *Vietnamese*. They have become a part of our culture.

Our word for coffee is Cà Phê (pronounced ca-fe). We have a penchant for baguettes for breakfast, but we spread them with chili paste rather than jam. We have also developed new ways to serve coffee. Sometimes it is roasted with fish sauce. In Hanoi, they have a local variety with whipped egg yolk.

Less physically tangible, but no less important, is Vietnam's long inter-connected history and trading links with our neighbors across Southeast Asia. Today, that familiarity is manifesting itself through increasing M&A and joint ventures between Vietnamese and Thai companies—the latter trying to escape low growth at home by expanding into faster-growing countries like Myanmar and Vietnam.

Then there is the very large neighbor to the north. There have been countless books about Vietnam's history and relationship with China. Mao Zedong once described it as being as "close as lips and teeth."

For one long period of time, it was even closer than that. Vietnam was consumed by China and ended up inside its body politic. The Han Dynasty colonized the country in the second century BC and stayed for almost a thousand years. Even after that, Vietnam continued paying tribute to China's emperors and used its script until well into the seventeenth century.

The Vietnamese are steeped in Chinese history and culture. But the country's history has also been defined by a battle for independence and a distinct cultural identity.

We are proud of our civilization and rightly so. It is this determination to be self-governing that explains why Vietnam is only now making that seismic shift in economic development—some decades later than East Asian peers. Vietnam's determination to shake off the French after World War II is well known, and what happened next represents one of the great tragedies of the 20th century.

The conflict that Americans call the Vietnam War and the Vietnamese call the War of American Aggression only ended as recently as 1975. It is interesting that America's Public Broadcasting System (PBS) TV network recently broadcast a critically acclaimed seventeen-hour-long documentary series about the war. It shows how the US is finally coming to terms with the terrible psychological rift the war caused among its own people.

One particularly striking episode was called "Riding the Tiger," which explained how the American people got sucked into the war in the first place. In his inauguration speech, President John F. Kennedy famously warned that those "who foolishly sought power by riding the back of the tiger ended up inside."

Little did he realize that it would be American morale that got devoured instead. But it was Vietnam that was punished for that perceived national humiliation.

The war left Vietnam in physical and economic ruins. American bombs had destroyed most of the country's rail infrastructure, bridges, roads, and canals. Over the next decade, hundreds of Vietnamese farmers died from unexploded landmines and bombs. Many of the bombs lay hidden underwater in paddy fields.

Millions of acres of forest had been defoliated by the toxic Agent Orange. The government estimated that more than half of the country's villages had been destroyed. The Americans' departure created more than ten million internal refugees, one million war widows, more than 750,000 orphans, 350,000 disabled war veterans, and three million people unemployed.

To say the economy was badly shaken would be a massive understatement. Liberation Day itself had been a time of joyous celebration for many, but political reunification was accompanied by economic chaos and internment.

Over the next two decades, two million people left the country— roughly 4 percent of the overall population. Nearly everyone in the South knew someone who lost their property, fled abroad, or was sent to re-education camps.

At peace talks in Paris, the US agreed to pay $3.25 billion in reconstruction aid to rebuild the infrastructure it had destroyed. Perhaps it could have panned out like the Marshall Plan, which helped turn Germany and Japan into economic powerhouses after World War II. But America never honored that promise. Instead, it imposed economic sanctions and a trade embargo. The US also demanded repayment for the millions of dollars it had lent the old Saigon regime.

The trade embargo was especially painful. It not only prevented Vietnamese businesses from buying US products but also those from elsewhere, since many other nations yielded to US pressure to boycott Vietnam. As the next chapter of this book explains, my father had to improvise constantly just to get basic parts and raw materials for his first businesses because it was impossible to import any.

No economy could have prospered under these conditions. In fact, Vietnam barely survived. It tried Soviet-style central economic planning and all peasant farmers were forced to work in agricultural cooperatives and hand over their crops to the state.

The policy had a predictable result; farmers had little incentive to produce crops if their families did not directly benefit from their hard work. As a result, agricultural productivity and food yields decreased, creating mass shortages.

Today, Vietnam is the world's third-largest rice exporter after India and Thailand. In the immediate postwar years, however, the situation was so bad that rice had to be imported.

Inflation raged at up to 900 percent. The government changed currency three times.

Đổi Mới

By the early 1980s, the government was forced to liberalize the economy, and it started allowing farmers to sell surplus produce. Capitalist economics were beginning to make a comeback. In the mid-1980s, the government adopted a policy called Đổi Mới (reforms), which it officially billed as "a market economy with socialist orientation."

It was very similar to China's open-door policy in 1979 and marked a pivotal point for the country. In 1989, there were a whole series of initiatives, which not only officially sanctioned private businesses again but also gave them the beginnings of a legal framework, which would allow them to flourish.

Some 45,000 private enterprises were registered once the law on private enterprises was enacted in 1991. Around the same time, the number of state-owned enterprises (SOEs) dropped from 12,000 to 6,300.

I started noticing many changes in the 1990s. For the first time, there were foreign brands in the stores, although at this point a lot of these brands were fakes rather than a real Gucci or Prada handbag. This only really started to change in the early 2010s.

Politically, the tension between the government and the US was starting to thaw. One major turning point came in 1994 when US President Bill Clinton finally ended the trade embargo, which had stifled Vietnam's economic development for twenty years.

The World Bank, the International Monetary Fund, and private investors began to view Vietnam as worthy of investment. The economy started growing by an average of 8 percent a year. Soon Vietnam was one of the world's biggest exporters of rice again. Thirty years after reunification, Vietnam joined the international community of market-driven economies. In 1997, Vietnam was admitted as a member of the United Nations.

During this time, Vietnam made great progress in reducing poverty, notwithstanding all the difficulties and the trade embargo. In 1975, 70 percent of Vietnamese people lived below the official poverty line.

By 1992, it was 58 percent. By 2000, only 32 percent lived below the poverty line, and by 2017 it was below 7 percent, a significant improvement. Education and health care also improved dramatically.

The government constructed a network of primary and secondary schools in every community. The country had a basic structure of health care delivered to citizens at no cost.

Today, Vietnam has a very high literacy rate of 94.5 percent and is still investing up to 23 percent of its budget on education. It is paying dividends and is another key reason why the country is being so assiduously courted by multinationals and financial investors.

Teething Troubles

At the turn of the century, Vietnam was going great guns. The rate of economic and political change was breathtaking. In 2006, it was capped by Vietnam's accession to the World Trade Organization.

Between 2000 and 2004, ninety thousand private enterprises were registered with total capital equal to $13 billion. This amount was much higher than the Foreign Direct Investment (FDI) Vietnam received during this period and five times higher than the whole of the previous decade.

The turning point came in 2006 when Merrill Lynch published a widely disseminated piece of research announcing that Vietnam was a "ten-year buy." The US bank concluded that wealth was being created at a "turbo-charged rate" as the population rapidly swapped "their bikes for BMWs." The hype built rapidly, and the investment floodgates opened.

In 2007, Vietnam received net foreign inflows of $17 billion. Investors were right about Vietnam's long-term potential, but over the short-term, the country simply could not cope with this tsunami of money.

To put it into context, the benchmark stock market index—the VN Index—was worth just $1.1 billion at the beginning of 2006 and comprised thirty-five listed stocks. Vietnam's overall GDP stood at $66.37 billion that same year.

Unsurprisingly, it all ended badly. After quadrupling in the space of one year, the VN Index collapsed, and by 2009 it had dropped from a peak of 1170 to below 240. As investors fled and the tide went out, the shallow sands underpinning the Vietnamese economy became clear.

Economic growth had been strong, but it had been of low quality, and as a result, several structural problems reared their heads. Specifically, reforms of the banking and state-owned sector had not kept pace with economic development. The government talked about equitization (Vietnam's word for privatization), but in reality, state-owned monoliths still controlled important sections of the economy, particularly traditional sectors such as heavy industry.

This situation became particularly apparent in the years after 2007, when the government responded to Vietnam's crash and the global financial crisis by pumping a lot of money into the economy via credit growth—$63 billion of it.[1] But as economists have frequently highlighted, much of this money ended up in the most inefficient parts of the state-owned sector, or in the real estate market, resulting in a banking crisis during 2011 and 2012.

That bad debt took a number of years to clear out. To make sure it does not happen again, the government has reinforced its commitment to reform the state-owned sector. It has embarked on an

---

1   PXP Vietnam Asset Management Correspondent, Nguyen Le Nguyen Phuong, email message to author, 2018.

ambitious equitization program and, as of early 2018, has lined up 240 companies, which it plans to restructure and, in many instances, sell off.

In recent years, the country's top leadership has launched the biggest anti-corruption fight in Vietnam's history, pledging to root it out. It is a problem which Vietnamese and foreigners alike complain about. According to Transparency International, Vietnam ranked 113 out of 176 countries in 2016 and then 107 out of 180 countries in 2017. These figures show a clear improvement. But if our country is to prosper we know it is something we must continue to face head on.

What Has Vietnam's History Taught It?

At the time this book was written, the Vietnamese were feeling very positive about the future. Indeed, market-research company Nielsen noted that Vietnamese consumers are the fifth-most confident in the whole world.

Pew Research Center also noted that the Vietnamese led the world in believing their country was better off than fifty years before. Some 88 percent responded "Yes," to this question when prompted, compared to 69 percent in second-place India.

One of the reasons for this is because Vietnam has hit a demographic sweet spot: 50 percent of the population is less than thirty-four years of age. A young, dynamic population is a marketer's dream. For them, the war signifies a piece of history they feel increasingly detached from.

They represent the social-media generation, who have had access to many more news sources. This gives them access to a more balanced view about what happened during the twentieth century. They do not want it to happen again.

Their ranks are also being swelled by the hundreds of thousands of overseas Vietnamese who are returning home, armed with a foreign education and the skills they want to bring to bear to help their homeland fulfill its potential. They are the children of those who fled after 1975.

In so many ways the wheel is coming full circle. Since the fall of Saigon in 1975, Vietnam has learned many valuable lessons and come such a long way. The country now realizes that centralized, top-down economic planning is not the most effective way to meet the needs of consumers, although as China has shown, it does have its uses when it comes to building physical infrastructure.

A truly vibrant economy requires laws that empower individuals and not just state-owned enterprises. The government understands the state-owned sector has not and will not be able to create the millions of jobs Vietnam needs each year to make sure its demographic explosion remains an asset not a liability.

Vietnam has an increasingly vibrant private sector. My father has not been the only one working hard to build a business since the mid-1980s.

As of 2018 there are several groups like THP with national scale, although overall, 90 percent of companies are small- to medium-sized enterprises (SMEs), or mom-and-pop outfits. According to Ministry of Planning and Investment figures, the domestic private sector accounts for 43.22 percent of the economy, compared to 25 percent back in 1995. State-owned enterprises have dropped from 50 percent to 28.69 percent over the same period.

And then there are the multinationals. They represent the remaining 28.09 percent of the economy and are a powerful force.

As China has moved up the value curve, Vietnam has taken its place in the manufacturing sector.

It now forms a key part of the global electronics supply chain, for example. One company, South Korea's Samsung, generated revenues of $46.3 billion from Vietnam in 2016, accounting for 20 percent of Vietnam's exports. When Đổi Mới began in 1986, exports totaled less than 10 percent of GDP. In 2016, they stood at 86 percent, a higher level than either Thailand or Malaysia.

Vietnam is a very outward-facing country and has eighteen free-trade agreements in place, or under discussion, with other countries. That might seem strange in the context of a long history of repelling invaders. But endless conflict has made us value tolerance even more.

There is a famous proverb, which states "dĩ hòa vi quý." In English it means "a soft answer turns away wrath."

Vietnam's history means that we pride ourselves on our friendliness and understanding, because we know these traits help to keep the peace. The country has had a long and difficult relationship with China. But Vietnam is very welcoming of Chinese tourists.

We are also very forgiving, because we have had to be so many times in our history in order to move forward. This is another reason why US tourists and companies are so readily welcomed.

Indeed, when former US President Barack Obama came to visit in 2016, many people took the day off work to see him. They lined the streets. They climbed the trees to get a better view. They believed he cared about improving Vietnamese-US relations.

But Vietnam is also a country that wants to avoid being swamped by the multinationals and foster its own companies, its own brands, and its own identity. For, if nothing else, the 2007 stock market crash taught the country just how fickle foreign investors can be.

Their money swept in and then it just as quickly swept out again. But the Vietnamese are naturally entrepreneurial people, and we landed back on our feet.

How far the Vietnamese/American relationship has come: enthusiastic crowds welcome former US President Barack Obama to Ho Chi Minh City, May 2016. Credit: Diego Azubel/EPA/Shutterstock

Vietnam is not a country that will get stuck in the middle-income trap that economists love to talk about when economies reach a certain level of development. The country's rise is also happening at a time when Asia is feeling increasingly confident on the world stage.

Our growth trajectory started later than our neighbors. But hopefully that later start will help us to avoid some of the pitfalls which bedeviled them, such as the Asian financial crisis in 1997.

It also means that while globalization has had a big impact in Vietnam, it will not become the dominant narrative as some fear. Asian values are already starting to reshape globalization in different ways. Vietnamese companies will hold their own with foreign ones.

CHAPTER 3

Nothing Is Impossible

THE PUSH AND PULL of globalization and localization have shaped Vietnam and, with it, THP. No company develops in a vacuum from the history of the country it operates in. And in the late 1970s when my father and mother were first starting to make their way in the world, that history was manifesting itself in two competing forces, which acted as yin and yang to each other.

Aspiring businessmen and women faced extreme challenges but also unique opportunities. These fed each other and drove both my parents to strive ever harder to create a successful business for themselves and their family. This chapter explains how.

As of 2018, THP is Vietnam's largest family-owned manufacturer in the fast-moving consumer goods category (FMCG), employing more than five thousand staff members nationwide. We have a 15 to 20 percent domestic market share, ranking alongside multinationals such as Coca-Cola and Japan's Suntory.

In terms of the healthy beverages subsector, THP leads the pack with a 50 percent market share.

Given where THP stands today, it is hard to imagine how difficult it must have been for my parents, Trần Quí Thanh and Phạm Thị Nụ, in the beginning. This is particularly the case for Vietnam's younger generation. They have grown up in a much richer and forward-looking country, which has embraced the market economy and is literally buzzing thanks to their dynamic attitude.

I come from the middle generation, sandwiched between them and my parents. In many ways, I think that makes me the lucky one. I was fortunate that I did not experience the horrors of the war, or its immediate aftermath, firsthand. But I did grow up during a time of scarcity, and because of that, I understand just how much hard work it takes to achieve success in life. I take nothing for granted, just like my parents.

I was thirteen years old when my father converted the Bến Thành Brewery Beverage Factory into Tân Hiệp Phát, later re-named the THP group. I grew up in the shadow of that transition. My family initially lived in the factory, and today we have an apartment on the top floor.

The company is an inseparable part of our family's DNA, and the second generation remains as committed to it today as the first generation was in the 1990s when my parents started building it up. They worked 'round the clock then. We all still do now.

It was not long before I began my own journey to support them, followed by my younger sister, Bích. During those formative years, I met thousands of THP workers and learned something of value from many of them. Nothing beats learning on the job, and I owe a lot of my ideas to that firsthand experience working on the factory floor.

My sister and I also owe a lot to our parents. Their story is an inspiration to us, and I would like to share a little of it because it is impossible to understand how THP became the company it is without getting to know them.

People often say great companies are the ones that understand their market and customers, but the truly great companies nearly always have an inspirational leader who creates and embodies the brand. Yet that does not mean the brand cannot survive when the leader is gone.

Apple is a perfect example of a company that has continued to bestride the tech world since Steve Jobs's death with its new CEO Tim Cook at the helm. Apple is still the world's most valuable company, but the company is what it is today because of Steve Jobs: his vision, his talent, and his steely determination.

A relationship built to last: Dr. Thanh and Madam Nu in the 1970s

My father and mother embody all three of these characteristics. In some ways they are yin and yang to each other. My father is an extremely logical person. A trained engineer, he can be fierce in his desire for perfection, although he is also a very good listener and teacher. He is a visionary, full of ideas and always eager to experiment. But at the same time, he also desires structure and control.

My mother is equally intelligent and a great salesperson. She is the soft power behind the company and has incredible people skills. She has always respected my father's business ideas, his leadership, and his appetite for risk and change.

She is someone who feels happiest when she can help others, and she is the one who always looks out for the company's employees. When she became sick in the last few years, they demonstrated their devotion to her by literally queuing up by her hospital bed.

My parents share many traits in common. There is no limit to their ambition, and they are relentless in pursuing their dreams. My father literally never gives up. Everything that they believe is encapsulated in THP's seven core values. The core value closest to my father's heart is the one which states, "Nothing is impossible. There are no limits to what we can accomplish."

Like all great entrepreneurs, my father is not afraid of failure. In fact, I would say he actively embraces it because he knows it will teach him valuable lessons, which will enable him to achieve even greater heights in the future. His drive does not come from a desire to be rich. Neither of my parents are motivated by money or lead a lavish lifestyle. They frequently carry no cash around with them.

If something catastrophic happened to THP, it would be the loss of the company they would mourn, not the riches that have come with it. Both of my parents started with nothing and would not be unnerved to return to that state. They are the kind of people who would simply pick themselves up and start again.

When they got married in 1979, they had to do just that, quite literally. Before they went on their honeymoon, my father had been living with his father. When they came back from the honeymoon, it was to a house that was empty except for two bowls and two pairs of chopsticks.

While they were away, my father's cousin had persuaded my grandfather to move in with him and bring all his possessions along, too. My grandfather had brought the boy up after his father died, but the cuckoo in the nest used my parents' wedding as an opportune time to make his move. Over the next five years, he completely drained my grandfather's retirement fund.

My father felt betrayed and angry by his father's departure, but one of his great talents is the ability to let go. Events like this have just made him stronger. By contrast, so many people end up suffering midlife crises because they want to make positive changes in their lives but fear losing all the material wealth they have accumulated if they trip up along the way.

My parents just move on. And this particular story had a happy ending when my grandfather eventually came back to live with them again. He grew to love my mother so much that he ended up regarding her as his daughter and not just his daughter-in-law. She is Catholic, and shortly before he died, he called in a priest to convert to her religion. It was a big deal for his large Buddhist family, but he did it out of respect for her.

Embracing change can be terrifying, but my parents believe there is nothing to fear. They have incorporated this belief into another one of THP's core values: "Today is better than yesterday, but not as good as tomorrow. Progress is never-ending; each day being a little better than the one before."

Life Is Difficult

My father is an entrepreneur and a successful tycoon. But was he born with the traits that made him that way—or did his childhood give them to him? Was it nature or nurture? It is an age-old debate, but one thing for sure is that his upbringing sharpened those traits.

The man who spent childhood nights facing down two giant hogs which were eyeing him up for their dinner was never going to be fazed by a company like Coca-Cola. And the pigs in question were not like the cute little porcine in the movie *Babe*. They were two hundred-kilogram monsters, fattened up on milk powder donated by Americans hoping to feed the children my father was living with at an orphanage for four years during the war years in the mid-1960s. His nights in the pigpen were a punishment for fighting, even though he had been standing up for another boy.

But it cut no ice with the nuns who ran the orphanage, situated in the mountains near Đà Lạt, a cold city in the Central Highlands. Despite the cool temperature, they dumped him in a pen wearing just a pair of shorts, a sleeveless T-shirt, and a pair of slippers. The slippers did not last long, as the pigs gobbled them up before he had a chance to climb onto a small platform that divided one pen from the next.

Fortunately, a kindly pig keeper gave him some rice to eat and straw to sleep on. The nuns bred pigs to provide income for the orphanage. Unsurprisingly, pork was featured heavily on the menu, if you can call it that. Breakfast, for example, was a lump of raw pork fat, the size of a man's fist, in a bowl of hot oily milk. Eating this dreadful concoction made some of the children retch. Others would bite into the fat too hard and the insides would spew out in a jet.

If ever my father tried to scoop out the lump of fat and hide it in the corner of the room, the nuns made him get down on all fours and eat it off the dusty floor using only his mouth, just like a pig. One time, he tried to take a bird's eye chili from the kitchen to liven his meal up. He was caught and made to eat a whole bowl in front of them.

My father's troubles at the orphanage made him resilient and taught him to overcome obstacles, including how to make the best of a bad situation. He was only ten years old when he arrived there in 1963.

He soon had to toughen up. Many of the other children had turned into thugs after being tormented by the nuns, and bullying was rife. A large percentage of those boys were not just orphans, but were also the discarded mixed-race offspring of American GIs: abandoned, rootless, and disparaged cultural anomalies.

My father was only at the orphanage in the first place because my grandfather decided to hide him there for fear his two stepbrothers would kill him for the inheritance his mother had left her three children. She had died when he was just nine after being struck by a coach as she dashed across a road in her haste to issue orders to workers at her trucking company.

My grandmother had considerable business acumen and had amassed a small fortune. Likewise, my grandfather was a successful businessman in the construction trade, and, together, my grandparents clearly passed on the business gene to their son.

My father showed early promise as a trader when his father made his annual visits to the orphanage. The nuns did not allow children to keep personal money, so my father pretended to hand over the small allowance his father gave him. However, he retained 20 percent for himself, hidden away in his sandal.

He also learned how to read his foe's psychology and play that to his own advantage, as having money was no use to him unless he could spend it on his favorite banh khot (savory mini rice pancakes) at a local stall. So, he told the nuns he wanted to attend a church service four to five kilometers away. They admired his spiritual devotion; he enjoyed his physical sustenance.

His father eventually decided to bring him back to Saigon. He was there during the 1968 Tet Offensive, fifty years exactly since the publication of this book. The smell of war and death was everywhere after the North Vietnamese Army launched a surprise assault on the city in the early hours of the Lunar New Year celebrations. Hand to hand fighting, the sound of gunfire, tanks, and bombs. Dead bodies littered the streets. It became the norm.

Such terrible times fostered a live-today, die-tomorrow mentality. The suffering that people witnessed or experienced had a big psychological impact, although young people, like my parents, were not aware of how it was affecting them at the time. Many students neglected their studies. Morals were looser. Fists were clenched tighter.

My father, however, said he managed to channel the increasingly "customary" aggression by learning martial arts such as Taekwondo and free boxing. As he progressed from belt to belt, he learned self-control. Instead of becoming a hotheaded young man, he became a coolheaded one instead.

When Saigon fell in 1975, my father was also in the city. In fact, his father's house was overrun with South Vietnamese soldiers who had chosen that part of the city to make their final stand. Luckily, they did not provide any resistance, otherwise it is highly unlikely he would be alive today.

By this point, he had graduated as a mechanical engineer from the Technical University of Saigon. He wanted to be an entrepreneur, but private industry was illegal, and Vietnam was in a chaotic state.

Private lands were being confiscated, central planning imposed, and rich business people were regarded as class enemies.

Many fled abroad or were sent away to developing areas for "re-education." Some were not released from internment camps until the late 1980s.

My parents' families did not escape unscathed. On my father's side, his half-brothers lost all their land. Their mother's legacy, which they had been so desperate to make sure my father did not get, was expropriated.

My mother's family had not been rich to start with and suffered even more than my father's because many of them lost their lives, not just their money. One of my uncles was killed in the war. Another one decided to flee in a boat. So did his sister, in another boat.

Many Vietnamese "Boat People" died at sea trying to reach neighboring Asian countries in the two decades after the war ended. According to UNHCR figures, about eight hundred thousand people made it to refugee camps.

They were not good odds, but many felt it was their only option to forge any kind of life for themselves. A similar tragedy has been unfolding in parts of the Middle East and Africa where millions of people have been leaving their countries in the hope of a better life. One thing I have always admired about my father and his childhood friend Uncle Tu, who heads R&D at THP, is that they both stayed and eventually prospered.

It was a different matter for my uncle and aunt. For most people, it took several attempts to save enough money to build a boat or pay for passage on one. It cost up to $20,000 in 2018 money. A huge amount at the time, payable in gold, the only currency that had any value.

My aunt set out with her husband and small son. Pirates overran their boat and it capsized. She was not a strong swimmer. Her husband only had the strength to hold onto her or their small son. He chose the child. The two of them survived; she did not.

My uncle and his wife decided to put their four oldest children on a boat, staying in Vietnam with their youngest three. One child starved to death on the boat and had to be given up to the sea. The rest survived and were eventually re-settled in the US. But many overseas Vietnamese people suffered post-traumatic stress disorder because of what they endured. It was not a well-known condition at the time, and they did not receive the counseling they needed. Two of those three surviving children committed suicide as adults.

Sadly, these kinds of stories are all too familiar to the Vietnamese refugees. The "Boat People" have become a bit of a forgotten topic to Westerners, but the war itself has not. When Westerners come to Vietnam, or meet Vietnamese people abroad, the war nearly always features somewhere in the conversation. Go to a bookstore and the shelves with books about Vietnam will be all about the war.

But it is not something the Vietnamese talk about among themselves. My parents and grandparents rarely mentioned it as I was growing up. Their attitude echoes how Western soldiers felt after World Wars I and II. After witnessing terrible events, the desire for normality is often very strong.

Creativity Flourishes in the Face of Deprivation

In the mid-to-late 1970s, my father was embarking on his working life, and his thoughts were focused on the future, not the past. He got a job at the Ministry of Mechanics and Metallurgy.

But he found it difficult to support himself on a government salary and in 1977 quietly started a small yeast business. But he was not quiet enough. My grandfather became extremely worried about what would become of my father now that private business was outlawed, so he decided to take matters into his own hands.

He told the police my father was running an illegal business. He also reported him to the electricity board, claiming he was using more than his allotted electricity quota.

The electricity board sent officials to investigate. My father could have ended up in a lot of trouble, but my mother had appeared on the scene by then and used her legendary negotiating skills to resolve the situation.

In his later years, my grandfather's concern switched from the possibility of prosecution to my father going bankrupt. He decided to intervene again, secretly giving my maternal grandfather a stash of gold to hand over to my father in the event his business failed.

But he was also not quite secret enough. Within a month, my father had found out and persuaded my maternal grandfather to invest the money in the business instead. His own father never discovered what happened.

Unfortunately, my grandfather continued to remain at loggerheads with my father about his business activities until he died in 1991.

My father's time at the police station also failed to deter his business ambitions. But for years afterward, it did mean he had to keep showing the electricity board he was not using more than his quota. So, he continued working crazy hours in a tiny little room, desperately trying to stay ahead of rampant inflation.

Many others were in the same boat, all trying to scrounge parts, because they could not import anything thanks to US sanctions. My father quickly learned two lessons, which have served him well in life. First, he understood that his biggest challenge was how to scale up and improve efficiency and in turn build market share. Second, he realized that to do this he would need to be innovative, as he simply could not buy the machinery he needed. He especially wanted centrifuge filters, which would allow him to produce larger batches of product at a cheaper cost.

Fortunately, my father's innate passion for all things mechanical quickly led him to the most innovative of solutions. The answer lay in the now disused US Army hammocks, which had been abandoned by the military when they hurriedly left at the end of the war. Much of the material found its way into Saigon's markets, and on close inspection, my father noticed it was made of high-grade nylon.

He recalled how American soldiers often used their hammocks to protect their weapons and keep them dry when they were crossing rivers. To the bewilderment of onlookers, my father tested his idea by taking a sip of water and forcing it through the fabric, using just the pressure from his mouth.

This became his secret centrifuge-filter process. The results were so promising that he rushed back to the market and bought all the remaining hammocks. He bought them for two reasons: (1) to ensure he had a sustainable nylon supply, and (2) to make sure his competitors could not copy him. Gaining a competitive advantage is crucial, but it is often temporary. After a lot of tinkering, he used the nylon to more than double his yields.

There was another reason why his competitive advantage was unlikely to last. The Vietnamese economy was rocked by waves of price instability and inflation. Economic conditions were terrible throughout the early- to-mid 1980s.

The government got into the practice of adopting a new currency every few years. Inflation was running around 300 percent, and the banks could not be trusted. Even if a business doubled or tripled its sales, it still lost money due to inflation.

In 1979, yeast prices also collapsed, forcing my father to pivot his business to a sugar- and fructose-processing operation instead. And this is how my mother's experience came into play; her first job had been selling sugar at a local wet market in Saigon.

One of the key issues in marketing is branding a product that is essentially no different from any other. Sugar is a commodity, and my mother was faced with numerous other stalls selling it at the same price as her.

Her solution was to apply the personal touch. She always remembered her customers' names. No sound is sweeter to most people.

She also made a note of how much sugar they bought and asked them whether they were satisfied with her service. From the surprised looks on their faces, she gathered she was alone in trying to forge a personal connection.

Later, she upgraded this into a proto customer-loyalty program. If they were loyal customers, she would give them a little extra sugar or a free sample of something else. Soon she was selling out her entire inventory every day.

It was my mother's idea to move from yeast to sugar after my parents got together. She was also the one who found the broken-down machinery my father was able to repair. Neither of them knew anything about sugar processing, but like all great entrepreneurs they viewed this as a challenge they could take apart and solve.

During the 1980s, the government also started turning a blind eye to private enterprise. My parents forged a partnership with a government company, which guaranteed a consistent supply of raw materials in return for a cut of the profits.

They also made sure they paid upfront, so the company knew they would not just run away with the stock. In turn, my parents have always said that they were fortunate to live and work in both the communist and capitalist system, because they have learned from both.

After a few years in the sugar business, they moved into alcohol distilling and then into beer. By now it was 1994, and the winds of reform were sweeping through Vietnam, legitimizing private businesses and creating multiple opportunities.

My parents' timing was perfect. Fast forward three years and THP had grown into a fast-growing business manufacturing beer.

The way things were: bottling drinks 1980s style

Life is starting to get less difficult: the Bến Thành Brewery-Beverage Factory, 1990s

My father then spotted an opportunity to buy a production line being scrapped by Saigon Alcohol Beer and Beverages Corp (Sabeco), one of Vietnam's largest state-owned companies. But it was not an easy acquisition. Sabeco did not want to help incubate a rival, so its managers broke up the production line and sold parts from different warehouses. My father made sure he was at every auction.

When Sabeco got wind of what he was doing, they tried to foil him by selling crucial components to scrapyards. My father and his men scoured every single one until they had what they needed. They even purchased bits of scrap metal they did not need for fear the scrapyard owners would bump the price up if they realized how desperate my father was for certain items.

Once THP had all the pieces, my father and his team had to work out how to put them back together again. He hired some Sabeco employees to help him; and after months of working round the clock, they got the production line up and running. They even managed to reduce the loss rate from 37 percent to about 2 or 3 percent. My father said he achieved it by never giving up. He also said Sabeco ended up respecting what he did.

That production line had the capacity to produce one billion liters of beer per year. My father dreamed of scaling it up to 300 billion liters. THP soon became the third-largest beer manufacturer by mass segmentation.

That line is still in operation today and has the largest capacity of any beverage manufacturer in Vietnam, although it no longer produces beer. The man overseeing it has also been with my father since the beginning. We call him Little Thanh, as he and my father share the same name. But the reality is that he has grown considerably in stature from working just one machine to running them all.

My family moved out of beer production in the first decade of the twenty-first century after my father calculated how much higher margins were on the soft drinks and teas THP had begun producing as well. Over the next decade, THP grew rapidly.

Between 2006 and 2009, the company grew by 400 percent. We launched a raft of new products, which I will explain in more detail in chapter 4, as they still form the bedrock of our output. Today, herbal tea is THP's best-selling product, with sports and energy drinks, soy milk, green tea, and bottled water not far behind.

Mutually Beneficial Partnerships

Since the turn of the century, THP has become one of Vietnam's leading private-sector companies. It has successfully ridden the wave of rising domestic consumption at home and taken its first steps to export abroad.

This fast growth should continue, given that disposable incomes are still on a very sharp upward curve. GDP per capita has nearly doubled since 2009 and stood at $2,200 in 2017. In the biggest cities it is above $5,000, the level where economic growth really starts to accelerate fast.

As I have already mentioned, the Western multinationals—Coca Cola, PepsiCo, Procter & Gamble, Nestlé—have all come marching into Vietnam to capitalize on one of Asia's fastest-growing and largest markets.

This book has extolled the virtues of local businesses, but economies benefit from having companies of all different sizes and from the interactions between them. So, the multinationals have been welcomed and done much to boost the economy.

> *Economies benefit from having companies of all different sizes and from the interactions between them. So, the multinationals have been welcomed and done much to boost the economy.*

THP is open to working with any company that can help promote our vision. And win-win does not mean a company has to be nice or has to compromise. It means the company needs to be clear about its strategic direction and find partners than can enhance or execute that. No company can operate alone forever. Partnering is a critical strategic skill. For example, we appreciate that THP's success has always been determined by its part-nerships with suppliers and distributors and contractors.

But the key is to create a solid platform at home first. This gives local companies the springboard to venture overseas. But local companies should never be afraid to step up onto the international stage. They should have the confidence to realize that no matter how small the country they come from is, they will have gained valuable insights from it, which may have eluded larger international companies that operate across many countries.

One thing my father has never lacked is confidence and, back in 2000, he not only established high goals but also made it clear he intended to out-compete the multinationals. This was his vision:

> *The THP Beverage Group aims to make a significant contribution to the success of Vietnam by creating the country's leading beverage brands. Our goal is to become one of the leading food and beverage companies in Asia while catering for global consumers.*

Note the audacity of that statement. In 2000, THP was not even among the leading food and beverage companies in Vietnam, let alone Asia. But like President John F. Kennedy's goal of sending a man to the moon and returning him safely to earth, my father intended to shoot for the stars, too.

THP's goal is to increase revenues from $500 million in 2016 to $1 billion in 2023 and $3 billion by 2027. We want to build our exports to 10 percent of the total by 2023 and hope to find a strategic partner that will help us to grow and share THP's vision together.

In the past, our suitors have largely been Western multinationals. And there is no reason why they might not be in the future. But one of the biggest trends in the world today is Asia's rise and the impact this is having on global business practices.

Many Asian companies have a similar background to ours and consequently think about their business operations in a different way from Western multinationals. They are often family-owned firms that value personal relationships.

They usually want to find a partner to help them access foreign markets just as THP does. But they generally do not want to take that partner over. Asian firms like joint ventures, and they tend to invest for the longer-term.

As Asia gets wealthier and its firms build up greater financial firepower, they are starting to push Western multinationals aside as well. Europe's demographic and internal issues have led several companies to beat a retreat and shut up shop across the region. It is Asian firms that are taking their place.

This dynamic has been very evident in Vietnam, where two of the biggest M&A deals in recent years saw a Thai firm replace a European one. In 2016, the building materials group LafargeHolcim sold its Vietnamese operations to Thailand's Siam City Cement for $524 million. That same year, France's Casino Group withdrew from Vietnam's retail sector after selling its supermarket chain, Big C, to Thailand's Central Group for $1.4 billion.

And then there is China and its famous "Going Global" strategy. Its companies are everywhere across the globe, but the government only started to encourage them to venture overseas once it was confident they had first built up a solid position at home.

It was very clever how it helped them clamber up the value chain. Western firms were so desperate to gain access to its 1.34 billion citizens that they agreed (readily or otherwise) to set up joint ventures with local partners and transfer their intellectual property and technology to them.

China learned quickly from that technology transfer. But while it has let foreign companies in, the government has made sure to keep control of key strategic industries and put a multitude of incentives and regulations in place to foster domestic champions. It is not

Amazon that controls online shopping in China, but Alibaba and JD.com. Citizens use Baidu to search online, not Google.

It also selectively blocks M&A deals. In 2009, it famously stopped Coca-Cola from buying Huiyuan Juice in what would have then been China's largest-ever foreign buyout. Today, Huiyuan Juice is still independent and ranks as China's largest fruit- and vegetable-juice manufacturer.

> *Vietnam does not quite have the same pulling power as China. It only has a population of 92.7 million, although as the fourteenth most-populous country in the world, it is not without considerable allure.*

Vietnam does not quite have the same pulling power as China. It only has a population of 96.34 million, although as the fourteenth most-populous country in the world, it is not without considerable allure.

The government has allowed multinationals to set up in the country without having to enter a joint venture, and it is allowing them to buy state-owned companies in full as well. But it is retaining control of strategic sectors, and it is doing a lot more to nurture private enterprise. By the end of the 2020s, a number of these national groups will likely have created successful regional footprints.

The Việt Kiều (overseas Vietnamese) will aid that growth. This common term refers to Vietnam's four-million-strong overseas diaspora, many of them former "Boat People." The government has been actively welcoming them back, because it knows the country will benefit from their talent and overseas training. Many are overjoyed to be reconnecting with their country.

During the 1980s, the term "vượt biên" (to cross the border) became a common term in Vietnam. As those people return and memories of the war fade into the background, perhaps those phrases will come to have a new meaning as we progress into the twenty-first century. To cross the border will assume a positive rather than a negative connotation, symbolizing Vietnam's growing confidence on the world stage rather than a flood of refugees.

Of course, my father has his own personal proverb about where he sees our company heading: "Great success comes to those who set sail for the sea," is his refrain. "No success comes to those who stay moored in the river."

Part II:
Five Steps to Success

How does someone take a good business idea, turn it into a viable company, and over time become a national, regional, or global champion? My parents created one of Vietnam's leading companies through a combination of talent, hard work, and simply being in the right place at the right time.

But there are several guiding principles all companies should abide by if they want to be successful. They may seem obvious, and yet so many companies fail to adhere to them. It normally catches up with them in the end. This part of the book explains what they are and how THP lives by them.

CHAPTER 4

Create Authentic Local Products

Winning brands are the Holy Grail for any company. Even better if companies can keep them flowing through a healthy product pipeline. Unfortunately, multinationals can easily fall far short when they try to create generic offerings for countries with very different cultural sensibilities.

By contrast, authentic local products are very hard to beat. This is because they are the only ones that truly adhere to the famous Four Ps—product, price, promotion, and place. If any one of the four is missing, the product will generally fail.

Of the four, place is often listed last, but it is dangerous to assume it is the least important. In fact, it is the other way around. And when it comes to understanding place, no companies are "better placed" than the local ones, which are indigenous to it.

This chapter outlines why each of the Four Ps is so important and then explains how THP has put them into practice, developing and sustaining three core brands: Number 1 Energy Drink, Zero Degree Green Tea, and Dr. Thanh Herbal Tea. But just because THP understands the importance of the Four Ps it does not mean we always get them right, so the chapter also includes a case study of one of THP's failures, Laser Beer.

Bottling success: THP's brand line-up

Product

A product is an item that satisfies a customer's need. It can be a tangible or an intangible one. Tangible products have an independent, physical existence, such as a TV. Intangible products cannot be touched but nevertheless have real value. They tend to be intellectual property, such as computer-operating systems.

Successful products are the ones that differentiate themselves from rivals in their specific target market. My father insists that every single THP product needs to have a functional benefit. This is what sets our company apart from the competition. Tasting good on its own is not enough. Nor is giving someone a sugar rush. Our company's drinks need to have a functional benefit as well.

Successful companies typically discover the magic differentiator by investing heavily in research and development (R&D). The head of this department at THP is Uncle Tu, my father's childhood friend who has been with the company since the beginning.

Luckily, local businesses have advantages over multinationals in leveraging customer insight. They are far more likely to interpret the research correctly because they are closer to it themselves.

Local companies also benefit from a more favorable risk/reward ratio when they launch new products, the lifeblood of any company. In Vietnam, it takes a multinational an average of two years to launch a new product. THP launched Dr. Thanh Herbal Tea in forty-five days. My father ran the project himself.

Local companies can get products to market much faster than multinationals because they are less bureaucratic and far more entrepreneurial. At face value, bringing a slew of new products to market might seem risky, but, actually, the reverse is true.

Local companies can act quickly, so they can easily remove products that are not working even if preliminary customer research had suggested they would. This minimizes losses and enables local companies to keep innovating. They can respond to success and failure much more quickly, learning from both to keep creating more of the kind of products consumers want.

Above all else, local companies typically only target their home market and can fully serve its needs. Multinationals rarely launch a product in one market alone. They make compromises to try to appeal across many.

Price

One of the most basic elements for any brand is its price, the second "P." The price determines the company's profit margin and has a profound impact on the marketing strategy it needs to deploy to sell it. When setting a price for any product, companies need to remain keenly attuned to the value customers attach to it, otherwise known as the *price-to-value ratio*. It is key for this particular "P."

Getting the price-to-value ratio wrong was the fundamental mistake THP made with Laser Beer in 2004. At that point, Heineken controlled the largest share of the premium beer market, and my father wanted to compete head-on by producing a draft beer in bottled form. Instead of going to a restaurant, consumers would be able to enjoy the fresh taste of beer at home.

He invested in aseptic bottling technology, which meant the beer did not need to be pasteurized and would retain its fresh taste. The target audience was high-income earners, and we believed they would be prepared to pay a premium. So, we priced Laser Beer at VND9,500 per bottle, compared to VND9,000 for a Heineken.

Our large investment meant we needed a pricing proposition for Laser Beer, but pricing above a competitor proved to be a challenge. Things then went from bad to worse when he found it hard to distribute the beer. Many restaurants had exclusivity contracts with competitors like Heineken, which prevented competing products from being distributed.

THP sued to overthrow the anti-competitive policies. The story was even picked up by the BBC. But it soon became clear the legal costs of the battle would outweigh the benefits. Soon after, the Vietnamese parliament introduced laws on anti-competitive practices. However, it took some years for resources to be allocated so they could be executed effectively.

We were also getting feedback that we had got the third "P," promotion, wrong as well. We marketed Laser Beer as "Bia tươi," which means fresh beer, but the affluent young drinkers we were targeting thought this was a product for low-income earners. They carried on ordering "Bia Dức" (German beer) or "Bia Tiệp" (Czech beer). Within eight months it was clear that Laser Beer was a failure, and we withdrew it from the market.

Promotion

As a product is being readied for launch, the third "P"—promotion—kicks in. It is no good having a great product if nobody knows about it. Promotion embraces all methods of persuasion, which a marketer uses to motivate customers to buy the product. It comprises elements such as advertising, public relations, and sales promotion.

These days, social media represents a growing share of any company's promotion budget, particularly when it comes to targeting Millennials (born after 1980) and Generation Z (born after 1995). However, Vietnam is a fairly traditional market, although this is changing fast. TV is still the lead medium.

As a result, THP still spends about 60 to 70 percent of its advertising budget on TV. In developed countries like the US, companies typically spend about 40 percent or less, because the market has become so fragmented. Western consumers have multiple TV channels to choose from, and many have switched to streaming services like Netflix where there are very few adverts.

Advertisers in Vietnam's consumer-goods sector also need to take a second consideration into account. They not only have to persuade the end consumer to buy their product but also the vendor.

In developed markets, consumers generally walk into a convenience store or supermarket to pick up a soft drink. FMCG companies consequently sell to a limited number of big distributors that control the market in that country and can carry multiple lines due to the large size of their stores.

Not so in Vietnam, where street vendors abound: bicycling around the towns and cities or sitting on street corners with their cart. There are millions of them. And unlike 7-Eleven or Walmart, they cannot carry too much stock. They can carry a maximum of fifteen different beverage products compared to two hundred in a supermarket. Making sure they have THP's products is key.

A third consideration is how much a company should spend on advertising. Many companies make false savings by trying to cut down on their advertising and marketing budgets. THP has never done this. Right from the beginning, my father understood the need to go out and sell his products and has always engaged the world's best marketers to help him do so.

For many years we used Ogilvy and Mather, Publicis, and, more recently, Dentsu. We never skimped on hiring the best talent to help us marry local insight with international marketing standards, even when we were a much smaller company than the multinationals we were competing against. In the early days, my father would religiously study how much money the multinationals were spending on their advertising campaigns and make sure THP did the same.

In getting their message across, local companies have several key advantages. Firstly, many MNCs still do not localize their advertisements enough. They will have regional advertising plans, which treat Asia differently from Europe and the US. But they do not always go that one step further and target individual countries.

Their brand ambassadors are often international figures. It feels far more authentic when a local company uses a domestic one. THP has put this to good effect in its most recent advertising campaigns, which are fronted by some of Vietnam's leading stars in their fields.

Secondly, local companies are often family owned, and their founders are well-known local figures themselves. It also helps that my father is a naturally ebullient character. Every year on October 15, for example, we hold a THP Anniversary Day when we gather the entire organization and their families together to celebrate the company.

My father is known for his flamboyant entrances onto the stage: one year on an elephant, one year riding a tank, one year dressed as a cowboy on a white horse. In this regard, he is a showman in the tradition of Apple's Steve Jobs, who always used to stride onto the stage in his black turtleneck, or Virgin's Richard Branson, whose action-man exploits included traversing the Atlantic in a balloon. Branson once said that he spends a quarter of his time devising marketing and promotional stunts for his company. It is generally money well spent.

I am carrying on the family tradition. At this year's THP Anniversary Day, I went on stage wearing an áo dài (traditional Vietnamese dress) decorated with hand-embroidered motifs of our main brands. I then sang a song "Hương sắc cõi tiên," which translates as "Tastes of the Realm." The song was written by some of our IT staff and is about the nine different herbs in Dr. Thanh Herbal Tea.

This plays into my marketing role, and I have been exploring novel ways to extend our message and reach our customers. One example is the problem page I set up on my father's personal website (www.tranquithanh.com). My father loves giving out advice, particularly if he can use one of his many proverbs to emphasize a point.

Sharing his experiences is important to my father. It also helps achieve one of THP's strategic goals to benefit the local community and country as well as the bottom line. Aspiring entrepreneurs have a channel to seek advice, and by printing their letters on the problem page, a wider audience can benefit as well.

In 2017, I took the idea one step further and established a networking event for all our suppliers. We held a one-day seminar at the end of September. Leading figures from THP shared their experience and practical tips and then answered questions across the whole gamut of the company's operations—from sourcing and distribution to marketing, crisis management, and family-business management.

I also recently launched a cooking show on Vietnamese TV. The recipes are based on the ingredients and herbs we use in our drinks. It has been a great success and really enhances our company's name in a more indirect way than a traditional advertisement.

It also provides a great forum for the women depicted on the show. We consciously choose women from different walks of life such as a housewife or a career woman or someone who is trying to juggle both roles to appear on the show. Each week, they discuss and solve a particular problem they are facing as they prepare the different dishes.

Place

The most important "P" has been left for last, and it is the one that deserves the most elaborating on. Creating a successful product hinges on understanding the place it comes from or is being sold to, particularly in the FMCG sector. Product availability is one of the key success factors. The traditional definition of place is the provision of a product at a location that is convenient for consumers to access.

Historically, this meant a physical store or outlet, but has increasingly become an online or virtual location.

Yet there is another, more important connotation to place—and it is very easy to lose sight of it in our virtual, connected world. As outlined in part I, some consumers pay very close attention to the place where a company or product is from, because they want to support their local community. This trend is becoming particularly noticeable in developed markets.

In developing markets, research shows that place is important, too, but for slightly different reasons. Here, national pride plays an important role. This was demonstrated when research company Nielsen conducted a Global Brand-Origin survey in 2016, polling more than thirty thousand consumers across sixty-one countries. It found that respondents in Asia and the Pacific and respondents in Africa and the Middle East were far more likely to cite origin as the most important selection factor (respectively, 33 and 32 percent on average) than other parts of the world.

But on a day-to-day basis, most people do not realize how much attention they are paying to place. For instance, when someone walks into a KFC branch in Hanoi he or she probably does not care how many global outlets the company has. The decision to eat there will hinge on how that person feels about the brand in competition with other eateries in the vicinity.

The factors underpinning consumer decisions are complicated and often subconscious. But they boil down to an individual making a purchasing decision at a particular place and moment in time. If other people make that same purchasing decision multiple times over, then the company in question is onto a winner and may want to scale up. Tapping into those subconscious desires is the key to success.

These days, multinationals try very hard to make their global brands the preferred local brand wherever that may be. They fine-tune their products and their branding messages to have maximum impact based on a target nation's language, culture, and environment. And there is a term for it too: *global localization* (sometimes called glocalization).

Firms can choose to localize everything from their advertising campaigns and product packaging to the product itself. When this trend first started in the 1980s, it involved very basic operational changes such as translating generic branding materials into local languages. But by the early 1990s, it expanded into adjusting products and services to suit local tastes and culture, as well.

McDonalds was one of the early pioneers as it ramped up its international expansion during that decade. In India, where cows are sacred, it sold hamburgers made with lamb and other non-beef products. In China and other Asian countries, McDonalds added rice to its menus. The restaurant chain worked hard to use local advertising, social media, and publicity outlets to encourage local receptivity toward its products.

However, even the most successful multinationals do not always realize when they are ruffling national feathers. Starbucks is a good example of how things can go wrong despite the fact it got so many things right when it entered China. For example, it correctly aligned its product offerings to local tastes—a green-tea Frappuccino anyone?

Starbucks understood that it would be more readily accepted if it adapted to the country's teahouse culture, which has prevailed for thousands of years. The company realized that success was less about selling coffee than creating a comfortable "third place" as an alternative to home and work for a growing population of young entrepreneurs to frequent.

The Seattle-based company's branding was also attentive to the most fundamental aspect of Chinese culture: the family. In fact, Starbucks built its entire Chinese presence around it. It welcomes employees' parents (called "partners") at annual Partner Family Forums where the company shares news about its operations and future plans.

It also launched other forums such as the Starbucks China Parent Care Program, which provides health insurance for the most elderly parents. This program is particularly liked, because it provides direct security to families. It is said to have done wonders for employee retention, which reduces recruitment and training costs.

But Starbucks stumbled when it placed profit over place and opened a branch in China's six-hundred-year-old Forbidden City. The local authorities had initially approved the outlet in addition to other vendors. But Starbucks ended up having to shut down its Forbidden City outlet down after local concerns about commercial activity at China's most important cultural-heritage site gathered a head of steam (and not the type that froths the coffee).

One very important lesson for multinationals is to take heed of local activism. It can often be decisive in prompting a national push back against global companies. No amount of promotion or advertising or local accommodation will prevail if a society feels its cultural identity is being trampled over. In China's case, the country had not only reached a level of development where there was a big enough middle class to care about issues such as heritage but also one where the nation itself was starting to want to assert its cultural identity on the global stage.

The kind of resentment and reputational damage Starbucks evoked can be hard to reverse. But when it is done right, global localization allows organizations to appeal to a wider audience, build market share across many countries, and learn valuable lessons about product design and customer service that can be applied far and wide.

> *When it is done right, global localization allows organizations to appeal to a wider audience, build market share across many countries, and learn valuable lessons about product design and customer service that can be applied far and wide.*

Number 1 Energy Drink

My father turned global localization to his advantage when he developed the first of THP's three core brands in 2001: Number 1 Energy Drink. At that point, he was looking for new avenues to diversify away from beer, where margins are lower than other kinds of drinks. (This is partly because of higher taxes and partly because it costs more to produce beer, as it needs to be fermented for twenty or more days and incurs other costs relating to storage.)

Red Bull had already come to Vietnam. But my father thought it was a typical example of an international company trying to impose a generic brand across many different countries, albeit one which has some historic links to our country. Urban legend has it that glucuronolactone, one of the ingredients in many energy drinks, was first developed by the American government to help GIs stay awake during Vietnam War.

Red Bull itself was the brainchild of an Austrian industrialist, Dietrich Mateschitz. But he got his inspiration from Vietnam's neighbor, Thailand, and an energy drink called Krating Daeng (Red Bull), which was popular among manual workers. In turn, Krating

Daeng was based on Lipovitan, a Japanese energy drink developed by a pharmaceutical company during the mid-1960s and sold in small, brown, medicinal bottles. It was a favorite of that country's famously hardworking salarymen and is still sold in those distinctive bottles today, including in Vietnam.

The history of the energy-drinks sector shows how brands typically derive inspiration from each another, with each individual brand applying a unique twist, which sets it on its own distinctive path. Mateschitz's talent was to re-configure Red Bull for Western tastes and then turn it into the world's first truly globalized energy drink.

My father's genius was to spot this trend early and develop a similar brand that better suited the Vietnamese palate. In particular, he thought Red Bull was too strong and too sweet.

THP's Number 1 Energy Drink has a tangier flavor. It contains vitamin B3, which aids the conversion to glucose; taurine, which enhances absorption and helps regulate heartbeat and energy levels; inositol, which aids the nervous system and serotonin modulation; and caffeine, which stimulates the nervous system.

He also thought Red Bull got the second "P" wrong as well: price. He thought it was too expensive for Vietnam's then-GDP per capita.

His solution was to ditch the kind of disposable can Red Bull was using and use a glass bottle that could be recycled. This meant consumers would not need to pay for the cost of the packaging, and my father would be able to sell his product for a cheaper price and still make a decent margin.

So, my father thought he had the product, price, and place ticked off the list. He also had a nationwide distribution system in place to sell his new drink thanks to his beer franchise. Now all he needed was to get the final "P" right: promotion.

Earlier in the chapter, I highlighted how THP always works with the best creative minds to develop marketing campaigns for our products. Nevertheless, one of the campaigns my father is most proud of is the one he personally developed for Number 1 Energy Drink. In the run-up to launch, THP ran a series of quick-fire adverts across all forms of media (TV, print, billboard) stating, "Number 1 is coming to Vietnam."

But there was no explanation about what Number 1 was. Everyone was curious. Quite a few people wondered whether it meant the CIA was coming back.

At one point there was even talk in government circles that Number 1 needed to be banned, because it must be an American company up to something crazy. This mind-set tells you a lot about my country's underlying attitude to the US at the time. There was still a lingering fear about the power and activities of America Inc.

Just before the product went on sale, we ran a full-length TV advertisement and revealed who was actually coming. And it *was* an American—of sorts.

The advert opens with a scene from the Mojave Desert in California. Through the shimmering heat, a cowboy blows up the dust, riding his motorbike to the sound of Ennio Morricone's classic spaghetti Western music. He stops at a remote shack to quench his thirst on a bottle of Number 1. But the cowboy is ethnically Vietnamese and so is the beautiful woman who serves him.

This concept was partly used because my father wanted to create an international image for Number 1. It was also inspired by his love of the American Wild West. He would have loved to be that cowboy. Indeed, one of the first things visitors tend to notice when they come to his office are the many photos on the wall of him dressed as one. He admires cowboys' independence, grit, and frontier spirit—and he incorporated all of that into the brand.

The media campaign for Number 1 was so successful that demand rapidly outstripped supply. Trucks had to queue for up to a week at a time outside the factory, waiting for new stock to roll off the production line—because the distributors were desperate to get hold of the product. They could add their own big, fat margin, because demand was so high.

My father was also very clever in that he managed to outsmart Coca-Cola and PepsiCo, and this gave the brand crucial breathing space to find its feet. Some years later, one of Coke's executives told us they had once held a meeting in Thailand, and the subject of our energy drink had come up. They concluded that we would fail since THP had no prior experience outside the beer sector.

Consequently, they did not pay us much attention. My father aided their misguided view by cultivating the impression of a small-scale operation whenever he met their representatives at trade fairs.

For example, one Coke executive told him it was suicide to sell energy drinks in a glass bottle and wondered how THP would process five thousand cases of empty glass bottles. My father countered that he "couldn't possibly be producing that kind of volume since he didn't have the capital." The reality was that THP was already producing much more than that.

Once Coca-Cola and PepsiCo realized their error, they tried to stop their distributors from selling Number 1. But they failed on two counts. First, Number 1 is not a carbonated drink, so they could not argue it was a direct rival. But more importantly, our distributors were locked in. They wanted to sell the drink anyway, because it was very profitable for them. And by this stage they had contracts with

THP, which they could not easily walk away from. In fact, this is where the use of glass bottles really came into its own. The distributors had paid a deposit for the bottles and they knew they would not get it back if they broke the contract.

Number 1 Energy Drink flourished. Within one year, it was honored as one of the top-ten beverage products in Southeast Asia, and as of 2018 our brand ambassador is Thanh Vu, Vietnam's first female ultramarathon runner.

Many of our competitors now have energy drinks in Vietnam, too, and it is a thriving market for all of us. Coke and PepsiCo themselves entered the energy-drinks segment in the first decade of the twenty-first century with Samurai (Coke) and Sting (PepsiCo).

Zero Degree Green Tea

Zero Degree Green Tea (Trà Xanh Không Độ) changed the tea-drinking habits of the Vietnamese people when it was launched in 2006, creating new demand. It was also one of the pioneering brands in the fast-growing ready-to-drink (RTD) tea segment, which has become increasingly popular.

Indeed, the growth of this industry subsector underlines the growing impact Asian history and culture is having on global consumers. As the region's companies develop an international footprint, they are bringing Asian tastes to a Western audience rather than the other way around.

When THP started developing a bottled cold tea, many industry observers thought the company was onto a loser. PepsiCo and Lipton had already collaborated on bottled green tea products in 2000 and again in 2002. But neither had worked, and in 2005, they withdrew from the market.

At the time it was assumed that consumers were simply not willing to pay for something they were accustomed to getting for free from any street stall (quán cóc) or high-class restaurant across the country. Iced tea is particularly popular in the south where the weather is much hotter. Northerners tend to prefer hot tea: sometimes so strong they joke that you can almost stand a toothpick in it.

And yet, many of the world's biggest beverage companies had already persuaded millions of consumers to buy bottles of a commodity they could easily get from simply turning on a tap. If consumers were willing to buy bottled water, why not bottled tea as well?

The key, as ever with any great brand, is product positioning. In Vietnam, THP had a head start because tea is an essential part of the country's national identity. Some of the tea bushes along the Chinese border are more than one thousand years old, and Vietnamese culture is (so to speak) steeped in it. Many folk songs ("Dân Ca Quan Họ") are about tea.

Unlike other Asian countries, where elaborate tea rituals are associated with the aristocracy, Vietnamese tea originated as an everyday peasant drink. Leaves would be plucked straight from the bush, boiled, and then served in an earthenware bowl to family and friends. Even today, the first thing a Vietnamese person will offer a visitor is a cup of tea.

PepsiCo and Lipton failed because they did not show the Vietnamese people why it was more beneficial to drink bottled tea instead. They just presented it as a new form of tea.

We have a saying in our country "Đáng đồng tiền, bát gạo." In English, this literally translates as, "It's worth spending money and trading rice." What it means is you may have to spend more money, but you will get good value or get your money's worth. The value

Zero Degree Green Tea offered consumers was stress reduction and convenience.

This fed into a very important trend. Everyone loves drinking tea, but as Vietnam gets richer and more urbanized, people have less time and inclination to make it themselves. This is particularly true of the young urban professionals who are the main target market for the product.

Second, by the middle of the first decade of the twenty-first century, awareness about health and well-being began to grow. Consumers began to move away from fizzy and sugar-laden carbonated drinks in favor of something offering greater health benefits. Tea is well known for its antioxidant properties.

Parents thought it would be good for their children, and today, many Vietnamese children go to school with a bottle of Zero Degree Green Tea in their lunch boxes. Urban professionals like it because it offers a more refreshing pick-me-up than water and a healthier alternative to fizzy drinks.

Tea is a very social, communal drink for my people. In fact, the expression "Trà chanh" has a double meaning. Its literal translation is "tea with fresh lemon," but it also now means to "hang out." Many young Vietnamese enjoy gathering together to drink tea over a plate of fresh roasted sunflower seeds.

In Vietnam, tea is typically drunk before or after meals, since most dishes, like pho, are very soup based. You will often see gaggles of friends or office workers drinking Zero Degree Green Tea together at lunchtime or after work.

My father thought he was onto a winner, and his trips to China and Japan had already shown him that similar products were working there. His customer insight meant he knew they would work in Vietnam too. Those trips also revealed that Chinese companies were selling cold tea in plastic bottles rather than the glass bottles PepsiCo and Lipton had been using.

He decided to make a big investment in PET bottles made of polyethylene terephthalate and aseptic technology, which keeps the whole process sterile and eliminates the need for preservatives. THP became the first company in Southeast Asia to invest in this kind of technology, purchasing a production line capable of producing twelve thousand bottles per hour.

But my father had also learned a valuable lesson from the launch of Number 1 Energy Drink. The product shortage had helped foster demand, but it had not been so good for THP's immediate bottom line. This time around—after getting the first test results back—he purchased a further five production lines capable of producing twenty-eight thousand bottles per hour. He also bought similar capacity for the pre-form bottles.

Then he set to work on the marketing campaign. One of the reasons why Zero Degree entered public consciousness so quickly was its jingle: "Không lo căng thắng mệt mỏi, giải nhiệt cuộc sống," or, in English, "Don't worry about stress. Cool down your life."

In Vietnamese, this runs off the tongue as easily as famous slogans such as, "Break me off a piece of that KitKat bar," do in English. Jingles have become very popular in the country as they once were in Western countries during the 1960s and 1970s. But the viral effect of social media has turbo-charged them into twenty-first century Vietnam.

Then, as it is now, Zero Degree's target market was youthful. This is not that surprising in the context of the country's demographics. As discussed in chapter 2, Vietnam has a population bulge.

According to Nielsen, Millennials, like myself, account for 30 percent of Vietnam's population. We are a twenty-seven-million-strong cohort who are forward-looking and dynamic. Millennials are not really interested in the scars of war and have a much more positive outlook on life.

Zero Degree's marketing and branding reflects this. The bottles are colorful (green and yellow) and so are the advertisements. Until 2017, commercials were fronted by Vietnam's biggest pop star, Son Tung. They featured a lot of singing and dancing with large numbers of young people. The vibe was fast, modern, and joyful—just as the consumers are.

That same year, we embarked on a new campaign, and it has proved to be very successful. We decided to take Zero Degree back to its roots so consumers could understand its DNA. The ads are shot in the tea fields where the product is plucked; they emphasize its natural origins, but they still feature lots of young people. As consumers' incomes rise, it has become common for young people to start traveling more, getting out of the city for the weekend with a group of friends. Driving around the tea fields is very popular.

Younger people are also far less interested in collective action than their elders, and they are no longer automatically deferential to them, either. They rate individuality.

This is one of the reasons why they are such big admirers of Western values. Zero Degree Green Tea speaks to their belief in feeling good about themselves. It tells them its cooling effects will restore inner harmony and balance to their hectic modern lives.

Chinese smartphone provider Oppo has also been very clever with its advertising campaigns targeting this demographic. Its advertisements highlight, often in very amusing ways, the generational divide between parents living in rural locations desperately trying to stay in touch with children who have moved to the cities.

Extended families are becoming a thing of the past, and children no longer feel the necessity to obey their parents or call them every day. Instead, their parents, usually the mother, strive to remain involved (some might say in control) in their children's lives by following them on social media instead.

When we launched Zero Degree Green Tea, its success was immediate, and many competitors jumped into the market after us. We exceeded our twelve-month sales target within two months. In 2006, we started off selling ten thousand cases per day. Today we sell over a hundred thousand.

Shortly after, PepsiCo was back with Lipton Pure, and later Tea+, while the Philippines Universal Robina Corp launched C2 and Coca-Cola introduced Tea Leaf. But THP had the first-mover advantage. Today, Zero Degree Green Tea still enjoys the largest market share in the green tea market category.

One other key consideration was pricing. The research we commissioned suggested that the optimum retail price should be VND5,500, and that the product would fail if it were priced at, say VND6,000. My father considered the research and concluded that the market for green tea was more elastic than the research seemed to recommend. THP's Zero Degree Green Tea was launched at VND6,000 and quickly became the market leader in the RTD green-tea space in Vietnam. It demonstrated, once again, that getting the Four Ps right and building a winning a brand is an art as well as a science.

Dr. Thanh Herbal Tea

After Zero Degree Green Tea's success, we turned our attention to other tea-related drinks, and just two years later in 2008 we launched

Dr. Thanh Herbal Tea. My father led the project himself, against the advice of some of his marketers who did not believe in the project. How wrong they were.

He chose to launch the drink in the run-up to Tết, the most important event of the year in the Vietnamese calendar. The reasoning was simple. One of the drink's key attributes is its ability to rebalance and detoxify the body after excessive eating—one of the main activities during Tết. It has a cooling effect (yin) to combat excess heat (yang) and dampness in the body, caused by too much oily and fatty food.

The Vietnamese people are well versed in Eastern medicine, and there is a very popular type of tea called trà atisô, or artichoke tea, which is renowned for its liver-cleansing properties. It is very common to buy bags of herbs from the TCM store, take them home, and boil them in water.

He decided to develop a drink, which retained all the attributes and goodness of TCM but was much more convenient—a very similar strategy to Zero Degree Green Tea. At the time the R&D team had 180 products under development, but my father instantly saw the benefits of developing one that helped to release inner heat. Spotting trends has always been his genius.

The drink he came up with uses nine traditional herbs that all have a cooling effect on the body. They include honeysuckle, which helps to reduce inflammation; chrysanthemum, which has a soothing and cooling effect; monk fruit (a small melon), which is particularly good for chest infections; spruce, also good for the chest and throat; licorice, which reduces liver fire; rosemary, which promotes wound healing and has anti-bacterial properties; and cucumber, which is also cooling.

The product was packaged in red (the yang color), and while the bottle itself has a modern shape and feel to it, the lettering and fonts feature a more traditional motif. He felt this would emphasize TCM's ancient lineage.

After some initial hesitation, he also agreed to put his own name on the drink and put his face on the bottle as a black and white line drawing. One big reason is because his first name, Thanh, also means cooling. It perfectly suited a brand message all about purity and cleaning by flushing out toxins.

Placing him in the black and white era enhanced the product's historical pedigree. And he agreed it was a good move, as he passionately believes the product gives him a healthy glow and there is a double meaning to the name.

From a marketing standpoint, putting his name on the brand had two further advantages. First, it would be easy for customers to remember, thereby helping sales. Second, we thought our own employees would feel an emotional tie to the brand and really put their hearts into making it a success.

When it came to the second "P," my father settled on the time-honored strategy of pitching the price at a premium. He also wanted to recoup his huge investment. He decided to charge VND8,400 for a 500ml bottle compared to an average of VND7,000 for other ready-to-drink teas.

How was he able to achieve this? Initial market research suggested consumers were willing to pay more because they believed our product had additional health benefits over standard drinks.

They were also reassured by THP's aseptic production technology because they knew the company would not only adhere to stringent hygiene and safety standards but would also be manufacturing a product with no need for industrial colorants or additives.

In addition, this technological efficiency meant THP could mass-produce Dr. Thanh Herbal Tea at an affordable price.

It was a win-win situation all round. Everyone at THP felt a huge sense of pride at being a market pioneer. And customers benefited, because here was a new product that offered health benefits, was manufactured to the highest international standards, and yet remained reasonably priced.

When it came to the third "P," promotion, my father invested heavily. In fact, in 2008 THP was the biggest advertiser in Vietnam, outranking Unilever for the first time. One thing about my father is that he always thinks big. He broke many rules when he launched Dr. Thanh Herbal Tea, but he succeeded. He spots trends early, can make quick decisions, and then just goes for it, very confidently.

He has been known to finish meetings by shouting out "Attack!" Everyone else in the meeting is then expected to follow suit. "Attack, Attack, Attack!"

So THP was everywhere: on billboards, on TV, in magazines, and all over social media. The new jingle was so popular that children were soon singing it in the playground. "Thanh lọc Cơ Thể, không lo bị nóng," or "When you feel inner heat, drink Dr. Thanh Tea." It is one of Vietnam's best-known jingles.

The target market was broader than either Number 1 Energy Drink or Zero Degree Green Tea had been. Initially, there was a slight tilt toward the older generation, who are more likely to suffer from indigestion and are more health conscious.

But the drink also appealed to stressed-out office workers relying on fast food because they have less time to cook. This gained further traction with younger people when they discovered that it mixes well with alcoholic drinks, since its herbs help to detoxify the liver and reduce the side effects of alcohol.

But above all else, Dr. Thanh Herbal Tea is all about family and the community. It celebrates family life and at no time is this sense of coming together more prominent than during Tết. A lot of people drink Dr. Thanh Herbal Tea after their family banquets, and it is very common to see bottles of it at weddings and other big social gatherings as well.

The advertising is unashamedly populist and plays on the theme of family and community. For example, one recent advertisement had a young man threaten to tear up his marriage certificate because his wife was lazy and spent her entire time playing video games rather than helping his mother with the cooking and cleaning. It played into a stereotype about southern women.

Northern women are viewed as strong and capable. The north is prone to natural disasters such as typhoons and flooding, which never affect the south.

As a result, northern women are commonly viewed as being far more organized. But after the wife in the advert drinks Dr. Thanh Herbal Tea, she is revitalized and full of energy. The marriage is saved, the mother-in-law is happy.

A second recent piece featured two rival bicycle drink vendors who suffer a crash after racing each other down the street. Both are seriously hurt, but after drinking a bottle of Dr. Thanh Herbal Tea that has fallen onto the road, they are not only able to dust themselves off but also decide to work together. They create a far more successful business than either of them had when they acted alone. The message is twofold. Dr. Thanh Herbal Tea not only physically cools the body but also takes the heat out of angry situations.

On a more general level, it makes Vietnamese consumers feel good because one of our national characteristics is that we like to think of ourselves as a helpful people.

This also relates to the country's geography and experience with natural disasters. Communities that do not work together cannot survive. We want to encourage that through our branding message.

And it has worked. Dr. Thanh Herbal Tea still holds a virtual monopoly in Vietnam's herbal tea category. In 2010, it joined Number 1 Energy Drink and Zero Degree Green Tea in being recognized as a national brand by the Vietnam Value program. This was set up by the government in 2003 to promote national brands and it has done a great job helping local companies understand why branding is so important.

In its 2016 annual report, Brand Finance said many Vietnamese companies still do not understand the role branding plays in shaping their future business. But it did note that Vietnam is the fifth-fastest-growing nation among the one hundred it surveys.

My father does not agree with this. He thinks most companies are well aware of how important branding is; they just do not know how to go about it or are afraid of spending the money to get in front of consumers.

In the past, Asian companies were not renowned for producing brands with global recognition, either. That is now changing. South Korea has Samsung and China has Lenovo. Vietnam wants to take its place on the top table as well. THP is helping to lead the way.

> *In the past, Asian companies were not renowned for producing brands with global recognition, either. That is now changing. South Korea has Samsung and China has Lenovo. Vietnam wants to take its place on the top table as well. THP is helping to lead the way.*

CHAPTER 5

Adhere to International Standards

WHEN A COMPANY SAYS it is working to international standards, it is generally referring to ones that have been tried and tested by global-market participants and become accepted as industry benchmarks. The best known are the ISO (International Organization for Standards) commercial and industrial standards, and in 1997 THP became the first alcohol beverage company in Vietnam to adopt them.

These standards help third parties to more easily understand what stage a company has reached or the quality of what it is offering. Adopting them should be a given. Who would not want to aspire to the best?

Yet some companies just want the certificate and are not really interested in pushing the boundaries of their knowledge. This has never been the case with THP. My father sought ISO certification because he wanted to learn how to become a better company.

He knew it would be tough to achieve given our stage of development at that time—and it was. But it was worth it, despite the months of five o'clock starts. Indeed, one of this book's key messages is that the best companies constantly strive to improve their standards and processes. There is always more to learn!

> *One of this book's key messages is that the best companies constantly strive to improve their standards and processes. There is always more to learn!*

However, making that leap up the value chain can be a daunting prospect for small businesses. Their founders and managers may lack the confidence to take a step into the unknown, particularly if their own money is at stake and they do not fully understand what the next steps involve.

Confidence is not something my father lacks. He brims with self-confidence and, as a result, is not afraid to surround himself with talented and successful people. He does not feel threatened by them. He actively seeks them out wherever he can around the world because he knows they will help him achieve his goals. But not everyone is blessed in this respect. It can be hard.

It can feel overwhelming for local companies when they first start thinking about hiring an international one to improve some aspect of their business. How does the local company even go about writing out the job specifications to choose between rival suitors?

And then there is the question of whether all the advice from international consultants makes sense. Surely the international company must know better than the local one, otherwise why bother hiring it in the first place? Sometimes this is the case, but not always.

However, it does make it harder for the local company to push back or even figure out which international company actually knows what it is talking about and which one does not. One thing we have learned at THP is to value international consultancies—but not give them free rein.

Time is money. No one understands this precept better than the consultancies themselves. They can take an awfully long time to produce reports stating the obvious. It is good to hire them, but it is twice as good to pin them down to very clear deliverables.

The fees they charge for their services can be extremely off-putting. The investment cost of their recommendations can be even more eye watering, particularly if the owners will be investing their own money. The key is to separate cost from value. The costs may appear high, but if the value is higher, then the investment is well justified.

My family tries to set no limit on our ambitions. We believe the sooner we embark on any journey, the quicker we will arrive at our destination. We do not hold back from making big investments in our company's future, and we always strive to adhere to the best international standards in doing so. In this chapter, I would like to explain how we have applied this ethos across different parts of our business operations.

Sourcing

The matter of raw materials is often one area where best-market practice means going local rather than international. First and foremost, local sourcing of raw materials, if available within the home country, is nearly always cheaper than international sourcing from a purely P&L perspective, because transport costs are lower. The logistics are far simpler and more direct.

Many multinationals also operate along these lines and source in-country. But where they differ is their tendency to try to squeeze their supply chains for every last ounce of profit. They do not regard their end suppliers as valued partners and try to use their own size to dominate and leverage cheaper pricing from them instead.

One of the main reasons for this is that supply-chain management is often remote. Regional or global headquarters often end up grappling with extremely long international chains, which have multiple branches and sub branches.

It increases bureaucracy and detaches one end from the other. Too often, the lack of a direct, personal relationship between the ultimate decision-maker and the people who produce their raw materials or manufacture their component parts, leads to exploitation, inadvertently or otherwise.

Some of the world's poorest farmers and factory workers end up becoming rounding errors on a spreadsheet within a cost center that is purely focused on profit maximization. One way to counter this is to promote accountability from the bottom up. Another is to ensure that local suppliers are paid a fair wage rather than the minimum one.

It is also important to put safeguards in place to prevent subcontractors from engaging in abusive working practices. Many of the world's tech companies learned this the hard way after a spate of suicides at factories in the Pearl River Delta in China in the early 2010s. One particularly bad example occurred over the course of 2010, when fourteen workers jumped to their deaths from the roofs of factories run by Foxconn, Apple's biggest supplier.

One of THP's biggest competitive advantages is its long-standing and deep relationship with Vietnamese farmers and international tropical-flavoring vendors. This is something my mother has always nurtured.

We always try to ensure we are maximizing these relationships. It is baked into the company's name: Tân Hiệp Phát (THP). "Tan" means new. "Hiep" means to come together. "Phát" means to develop. "Tân Hiệp Phát" means, "Together we grow." It is also the foundation of my parents' marriage. They started out as supplier and customer. They came together and grew as a couple.

There is also a second advantage when one local company—like a THP—buys from another. There are no language or cultural barriers. When there is a problem, the owner can also usually address the issue face-to-face rather than one step removed by phone or email.

> *We always try to ensure we are maximizing these relationships. It is baked into the company's name: Tân Hiệp Phát (THP). "Tân" means new. "Hiệp" means to come together. "Phát" means to develop. "Tân Hiệp Phát" means, "Together we grow."*

But THP's attitude is not driven by altruism. It is about creating a win-win scenario for both sides. This kind of working relationship will ultimately boost our profits. We always try to adhere to the definition of a supplier partnership provided by the Institute of Supply Management. It defines it thus:

> *A commitment over an extended time to work together to the mutual benefit of both parties: sharing relevant information and the risks and rewards of the relationship.*

We regard our suppliers as the procurement department's customers. We also have specially designated supplier relationship managers whose job is to make THP's supply-side relationships as productive as possible. They have monthly meetings with our suppliers and generate key performance indicators (KPIs), measuring performance against goals.

It is important for suppliers to feel they are an integral part of the procurement process. We must recognize their pain points, just as they recognize ours. As the ties between two partners get stronger, so do the strategic results. This is what creates a win-win partnership over the long term.

Many partnerships fall apart because they are not fifty-fifty; one side will always suspect the other of being predatory. When collaboration is combined with trust, both sides will also generally accept that, at any one point in time, one party may benefit more than the other.

The mutual benefits are well documented. When a management consultancy conducted an audit of our business processes, it demonstrated how businesses that adhere to this ethos could launch products 40 to 60 percent faster. Suppliers seek stability.

If they have it, they will be in a much better position to withstand periods of low demand and can respond more flexibly to periods of high demand. Furthermore, supply chains are only as strong as their weakest link. Instability threatens continuity of supply through stock outs and an inability to meet demand spikes.

Collaboration works best if the KPIs are clearly articulated, transparent, and based on a joint business strategy. Communication is key because it builds trust and avoids misunderstanding.

If THP fails to maintain excellent and ongoing communication with its supply chain, customers will suffer too. It is as simple as that. The more information we have, the more accurately we can forecast our ability to satisfy our customers.

Too many companies sabotage themselves by withholding information from their suppliers for fear of it leaking to a rival. For example, the retail industry often undermines collaboration by keeping its suppliers at a distance. If a company hides the metrics that suppliers must meet, then it cannot expect suppliers to hold themselves accountable.

Every year, THP's suppliers present the company with the fruits of their R&D: innovative technologies such as new flavors and concepts. That way we can do a better job deciding which to apply. We cannot innovate without them.

There are so many benefits to strategic supplier collaboration. Best practices can be shared throughout the supply chain. Defects and waste can be eliminated, thereby reducing costs. Transparency and better communication empowers every participant along the supply chain to exercise better judgment and to take ownership over results. A shared understanding of what the organization requires allows suppliers to anticipate and address problems before the organization is even aware of them.

Production

The meat and bones of almost any company is where, how, and when it manufactures its products. So many variables go into this decision, but as the chapter will show, THP always strives to keep bettering itself.

We are constantly on the lookout for new production methodologies, which will help make what we do more efficient. But we never want to lose sight of the fact that even though we have become more automated, our machines are still being operated by people who want to feel empowered by their work. As the world becomes ever more dependent on machines, it is very easy to lose sight of this.

One of the first decisions any company needs to make is where to base its manufacturing plant. Clearly the most cost-effective option is to be as close to customers as possible. Traditionally, food and beverage companies had to be close at hand because their goods were perishable. As cold-chain logistics developed, this became less of an issue.

But in recent years, Western consumers in particular have been a lot more conscious of the environmental costs of shipping food and drink around the world. They are increasingly looking local again.

White goods companies, on the other hand, still tend to find the lowest-cost country they can to manufacture or assemble their goods. If it is right next to the developed market they hope to sell into, even better! Mexico has such a relationship with the US.

Asia has been a low-cost manufacturing hub ever since Japan started booming in the 1960s, and now it is Vietnam's turn for all the reasons discussed in part I. Vietnam has a large, educated, and naturally industrious population. But it is still a low-cost one. This makes it a honey pot for multinationals.

The government has also been very proactive about encouraging such investment. It provides cheap land in zoned industrial parks with preferential tax rates and a host of other incentives. THP has taken full advantage of this and has grown in tandem with Vietnam's expanding number of industrial parks.

Between 2012 and 2018, we expanded from one to four factories. All three of our new factories are located in industrial parks. When the latest one is complete during the fourth quarter of 2018, the three new factories will have the same capacity as our original factory in Binh Duong Province, just north of Ho Chi Minh City.

When we set up there during the 1990s, the province had become a magnet for foreign multinationals. It was close enough to serve the city, but land was still plentiful and cheap. By 2004, Binh Duong had attracted the second-highest level of FDI in Vietnam.

Our headquarters is situated in Thuan An District, which is about fifteen kilometers from downtown Saigon and is, in fact, now zoned within the metropolitan area. At some point, the whole district is likely to be re-zoned for residential or commercial use rather than light industrial. This knowledge and the desire to establish a more even national footprint were the two driving forces that led to our new factory-development plan.

Even the most cursory glimpse at a map reveals what a long and slim country Vietnam is. Throw a lack of highways into this mix and logistics become difficult. But THP has always been determined to distribute its products to remote areas. So as the company got bigger, it made a lot of sense to establish factories elsewhere.

We chose our locations carefully. Being close to a good quality water supply is always one of the key considerations, since it costs a lot of money to treat sub-optimal water. It was also important to ensure there would be a steady enough supply of good water to support a factory over a fifty-year time frame.

We built our first new factory in the Kien Khe Industrial Park in Hà Nam Province. This is about fifty kilometers south of Hanoi in the Red River Delta, with water sourced from a nearby mountain spring. It began production in 2014—the year THP marked its twentieth anniversary.

This was also the year when production capacity hit one billion liters per annum: a staggering growth trajectory over two decades. Capacity had risen one thousand times from the original one million liters per year. When our third and final new factory opens at the Hau

Industrial Park in the Mekong River Delta later in 2018, capacity will have expanded to 2.4 billion liters per year.

Our second new factory is in the Chu Lai Open Economic Zone, close to Da Nang in the central province of Quang Nam. It opened in early 2017, and if its name sounds familiar, that is because Chu Lai was once a base for the US Marine Corps during the war.

The former American military airport was converted for civilian use in the middle of the first decade of the twenty-first century. For once, something positive emerged from the devastation, and the government gained a valuable building block to transform the area into an economic zone, which is lifting standards of living along the whole central coastal strip.

Setting up a manufacturing footprint across the country has helped THP become a truly national company in all aspects rather than a southern-owned one. The new factories are improving our logistics, providing work opportunities across the country, and helping take our brands to a new level. Few things inspire consumers with more confidence than the knowledge a company has invested in their area.

Even more important than the decision about where to locate the factory is the one concerning how to manufacture the product inside it. Right from the beginning, my father's main consideration was how best to scale up. He always knew that as THP got bigger it would only be able to compete with the multinationals by deploying the same or better technology.

Fortunately, he has always been passionate about this side of the business because of his mechanical leanings. He quickly realized he had to travel the world to source the best machinery. This might seem obvious, but at the time it took foresight and guts for a Vietnamese businessman, blinkered by years of a closed economy, to simply jump on a plane and take off.

But my father's entrepreneurial spirit and fascination with all things engineering meant that he was more than happy to travel far and wide and experiment with the best. Within years of founding THP in 1994, he had met engineers in Germany, Japan, Canada, and Australia. We eventually selected German-designed technology in the run-up to the launch of Zero Degree Green Tea in 2006. No other Southeast Asian company was using it at that time. Later, we introduced aseptic technology.

This technology means the whole bottling process is conducted in a sterile environment, using clean rooms, bacteria filters, and dry or steam heat. This not only maintains the maximum number of nutrients but also enables the products to be preservative-free because they keep for longer periods.

Staying at the forefront of new technology: Dr. Thanh Herbal Tea rolls off the fully automated production line

Deploying aseptic technology was a bold move. Many of our competitors thought it would financially ruin us, since one aseptic production line costs three times more than a conventional one. Our local factory workers were extremely nervous, because they had no experience with that level of automation.

The company's engineers were also apprehensive about going abroad and having to negotiate with foreign suppliers. But my father had no such qualms; once he decides an investment makes financial sense, he will always go for it—while making sure we get the technical support to execute it properly.

Even the people from Krones were surprised when he first rocked up to an international trade fair ready to roll. They were used to lower-ranking engineers doing the research and then reporting back to a board of directors before a decision was made. Here was a company founder, ready to invest a large sum of money.

But he had already done his homework, and one of the reasons he picked Krones was because they held a dominant market share supplying this kind of machinery to the beverage sector. Nonetheless, it was a steep learning curve, and it took three years before THP achieved acceptable yields for that first aseptic production line.

Aseptic technology has always been my father's pride and joy. To date, we have invested $300 million across seven aseptic lines. When all the current factories are operational, there will be ten lines, each capable of producing up to forty-eight thousand bottles per hour. It has been a worthwhile investment. It is a perfect example of the value outweighing the cost.

As well as being efficient, the technology also underpins and reinforces the health and safety benefits of THP's drinks. There is an environmental benefit too. The process is far more energy efficient and therefore reduces the amount of water needed.

Theoretically, Vietnam should not suffer shortages, as it has one of the highest number of renewable freshwater sources in the world.

However, bad management and uncontrolled development means this is no longer the case.

As such, one of the ways THP maintains international standards is by being conscious of its environmental footprint. We were, therefore, very keen to achieve ISO 14001: 2004 certification, which covers environment management.

As we have become more automated, we have also tried to keep our employees engaged with the machines they operate. Initially, we introduced 5S and Super 5S standards. These are Japanese standards—"seiri, seiton, seiso, seiketsu, and shitsuke"—which translate as "sort, straighten, shine, standardize, and sustain." It is a systemized approach to improving productivity by keeping the working environment clean, safe, and standardized across different areas.

In recent years, we have taken this one step further by introducing total productive maintenance (TPM) standards. Before this, we had one team of people operating the machines and another one fixing them. However, whenever a machine broke, the operators would typically blame the maintenance team for not fixing it properly, while the maintenance team would blame the operator for being careless.

TPM solves this problem by making the operator responsible for running and maintaining a machine. It empowers them by giving them ownership of their individual machine.

It also improves efficiency, because operators are also trained in preventative maintenance and are, therefore, always on the lookout for potential problems. At first, it was quite difficult to change the operators' mind-set. But it has worked and THP has now reached the AM4.5 standard.

Around the time my father introduced aseptic technology in 2006, he also began thinking about how to improve his warehouse management. My sister Bích was also very keen to improve this area, too. By this point, she had completed her studies and joined the family business. Her financial training gave her a keen eye for detail, and it was clear something needed to be done.

The company had become a lot bigger, but warehouse management had not kept pace. There was a huge amount of inventory that had not been counted for many years—and there was no rhyme or reason to where it was being stored.

Half the time we did not know where the stock was, making it difficult to do a proper stock count. My father was not reading many management reports either. He just looked at the levels for stock in, stock out, and remaining inventory.

So, we hired Australia's Logistic Bureau International to re-design THP's main factory and warehouse. We were conscious that there were many areas we could improve, including safety, efficiency, and the overall layout. We wanted to plan for a big expansion.

However, we ran into a snag. Binh Duong Province gets a lot of rain and the water table is always very high. This makes it prone to flooding and subsidence. We discovered it would be prohibitively expensive to introduce modern racking and conveyer belts because of the piling costs to support the warehouse floor.

Companies need to continually invest for the future, but it has to make economic sense. In this instance, my father did not think it was a smart way to spend his money. The value would not outweigh the cost. Therefore, at this factory the crates are still block stacked. There is far less automation than at our three new factories. Pallets are lifted by forklift truck and then onto the trucks.

One thing we did was completely overhaul our safety standards. This is something my father thought about for some time, but was unsure how to implement the new standards. It is something we now take very seriously. Flip flops are out. Hi-vis vests and hard hats are in.

Staff members are also no longer likely to see my father zooming around the warehouses on his motorbike, keeping an eye on everything. He used to know everyone's name as well, but with five thousand employees that is now impossible. Nevertheless, he does still try to remember as many names as he can—and you will still see him driving around, this time in a Lexus four-wheel drive.

Distribution

In Vietnam, the multinational beverage companies concentrate their sales on the six largest cities (Ho Chi Minh, Hanoi, Hai Phong, Can Tho, Khanh Hoa, and Da Nang). Why? Partly because the logistics make it more expensive to penetrate further inland and partly because market research firms such as AC Nielsen are based in the main cities. Multinationals depend on them for their statistics and research.

THP is a metric-driven company, as well, and we value our relationships with the research firms. Their insight is invaluable and an investment that is always worth making. But our penetration is far deeper than the multinationals in two respects.

First, we do not just analyze trends in urban conurbations where sales are concentrated. We seek to understand what people are thinking in the provinces, too. We also dig far deeper into people's lives than a focus group or in-depth consumer interview will ever do.

We actually move in with our customers, shadowing their every move (well *most* of them): observing their thoughts and behavior as they eat, sleep, work, and play. We really want to understand what makes the Vietnamese people tick and how that feeds back into the country's history, culture, folk tales, and proverbs.

Second, we have never been deterred by the logistical challenges of operating over an enormous and, at times, hilly and inhospitable terrain. Local companies all over the world have a similar mind-set where their national geography is concerned. It is a strategic advantage. The light may not burn so bright in the remotest areas, but it is nevertheless welcoming.

In Vietnam, the reality is that about 70 percent of the population lives in small towns and rural areas. So THP works extra hard to be their beverage of choice there. We compete for 100 percent of the market, whereas multinationals effectively compete for 30 percent.

There is a second advantage to this approach in rapidly urbanizing emerging- and frontier-market countries like Vietnam. We foster brand loyalty out in the provinces; then, as their populations migrate to the cities, they take those preferences with them.

We currently distribute our drinks to roughly 250,000 retail outlets through five hundred distributors and wholesalers. There are typically three main distribution channels in the FMCG sector:

1. *Wholesalers* buy in bulk and can generally sell wherever they choose to. This accounts for about 30 to 35 percent of THP's distribution business.

2. Then there are *distributors*, which enter into direct contracts with manufacturers and have non-compete clauses with rival companies. This accounts for about 60 to 65 percent of THP's business.

3. Finally, there is *Modern Trade*, which consists of supermarkets and hypermarkets. As of early 2018, this constitutes less than 10 percent of THP's business, but it is growing very fast.

Vietnam still has a lot of mom-and-pop stores and even more street carts for which the country is very famous. But this will change within a decade as the country embraces new ways of shopping.

Thai groups have been particularly active and have family-owned backgrounds much like THP. For example, the Chirathivat family's Central Group recently purchased the Big C chain, while Charoen Sirivadhanabhakdi's TCC Group now owns MM Mega Market.

The Ministry of Industry and Trade forecasts there will be 1,500 supermarkets in the country by 2020, up from 1,000 in 2017. This is likely to change the nature of THP's distribution model, which is currently based on pick up and pay (i.e., distributors and wholesalers pay for product at the time of sale). But it will not change the value, which THP places on the relationships it has with them.

Just like suppliers, they are critical partners to THP's success. No business can go it alone. Every company needs to make sure that products are available at the correct time, through the correct channel, and at the correct price. Only excellent collaborative and information-sharing relationships can reliably ensure this outcome.

This ethos also led to one of the hardest decisions my father ever had to make when my brother Dũng entered the distribution business after resigning as THP's sales director for Ho Chi Minh City. He did it without capital from my father. He got up every morning at four o'clock to open the warehouse himself, my father's warnings about 95 percent of businesses failing ringing in his ears. Most nights he did not come home till after midnight.

His business started well, and he was soon THP's largest distributor, making fat margins. He grew very fast and was managing hundreds of staff and dozens of trucks. This, in itself, was not a problem.

The issue was the lack of control systems he put in place to manage that growth. Soon my father was receiving a lot of complaints from other distributors. They said Dũng's staff were dumping product on the market.

Dũng was warned several times, and matters came to a head when a group of distributors provided hard evidence and threatened to sue. My father knew he had to treat all distributors equally and that if he allowed Dũng's business to continue breaking the rules, others would follow suit.

There was a family meeting, where Dũng acknowledged his mistakes and agreed to dismantle his business. He did not cry; he did not beg for another chance; he knew he had to pay the price for losing control. We all admired him for accepting his failure, and today he runs a successful collagen business.

Since the mid-2000s, we have completely professionalized our fleet-management and distribution practices. The government's infrastructure program has been a great help because it means there are more highways, which cuts journey times and enables us to use more of the larger forty-foot trucks.

We have also gradually improved our truck-maintenance standards. In the past, a truck would often have the logo of one model on the outside, but the inside would actually be a mishmash of all sorts of second-hand parts. Unfortunately, this state of affairs did not exist because the original parts had become worn out. They were simply being substituted for cheaper ones, to enable a number of palms to be greased along the way.

We always knew it would take a while to clean up this kind of under-the-table behavior. But we have been able to achieve it and today we are proud of our distribution network and the people who run it. It has been achieved thanks to a combination of diligence and the recruitment of new managers who have been trained to higher standards. As the next chapter will explain, putting the right controls in place is one of the key measures a company needs to think about as it expands.

CHAPTER 6

Govern Growth

MANY SMALL COMPANIES want to become bigger ones, but one of the most important lessons they need to learn is to not focus solely on growth. If they do not put the right IT systems and operational procedures in place to control it, they are very likely to come unstuck.

It was a lesson my brother learned the hard way with his trucking business, outlined in the previous chapter. Many emerging-market companies have had similar experiences on an even larger scale. Indeed, the Asian financial crisis, which began in 1997, was the direct result of uncontrolled corporate expansion into all sorts of unrelated business areas, fueled by short-term debt in a foreign currency.

Since the beginning of the decade, the International Finance Corporation (IFC) has spent a lot of time promoting corporate governance in Vietnam. It remains to be seen how many companies have taken its message on board.

In a fast-growing economy, it is all too easy for companies to believe their strong growth trajectory will continuously outstrip losses as a result of poor or nonexistent processes or governance. Companies become so fixated on capturing market share they do not realize they are creating a monster until it becomes too late, and they lose control of it.

THP's chief marketing officer, Stefan Reicherstorfer, says my father is quite unusual compared to many of the entrepreneurs he has worked with over the years. Stefan's view is that entrepreneurs typically have great vision, but far fewer have the matching discipline.

But transparency, control, and discipline are all very important to my father. He often says individual competency only accounts for 20 percent of the job and discipline the remaining 80 percent.

But he is not authoritarian for the sake of it. He wants to free up his own time by empowering other people, but he needs to ensure he can trust them first. This is also important because as companies get larger, loose controls leave them vulnerable to all kinds of fraudulent behavior. Getting rid of it has been one of the biggest changes and challenges THP has tackled since the turn of the century.

Unfortunately, petty bribery and kickbacks are deeply entrenched in many developing countries, so shedding them is a frustratingly slow process. We would not like to give anyone the impression that it has been an easy journey—because it has not.

It helps that the upper echelons of the Vietnamese government are now focused on cleaning up their own ranks, too. If Vietnam is successful, it will be one of the country's markers to upper middle-income status.

At THP, the need to start putting processes in place became clear by the late 1990s as growth really started to ramp up. Prior to that, everything had been centralized under my mother and father. They were signing off on every decision, and the paperwork had become overwhelming.

And "paperwork" is the operative word here, since Vietnam was and still is a country where bureaucrats remain wedded to stamping and chopping documents. Banks, for example, require documents to be signed by hand and in blue ink.

My father realized something needed to change, and he signed up for a management course with my mother and his childhood friend, Uncle Tu. This was when he first learned about ISO standards; he quickly decided THP needed to follow suit.

Implementing ISO was a very hard cultural change for the whole company. One of the most important steps in the ISO process lies in documenting what tasks each worker performs. This was particularly hard for some of THP's manual staff. They were used to operating machines, not pen and ink.

But it was an incredibly important first step in "professionalizing" the company. Once each worker's tasks and processes had been documented, it was possible to see where the gaps were and which workers were falling short.

THP also now had a blueprint to train everyone across the company to the same standard. The company was on its way to becoming the best-practices and processes-driven company it is today.

Keep Your Eye on IT

THP also uses technology to ensure transparency and consistency across the company. Since the 1990s, IT systems have revolutionized the ways businesses are managed.

But they came late to Vietnam, and it was only in 1997 that my father purchased his first computer: a laptop. No one else at THP had one then.

This was also a time when the currency was still all over the place, so the computer's cost—just like everything else of value in the country—would have been considered in terms of how many gold bars it represented. Plus, owning a computer is not much use if you do not even know how to switch it on.

So, my father organized IT training for senior staff members. Another key theme of this book is the emphasis THP places on self-improvement and training—something that will be explored in the next two chapters.

Once again, he quickly concluded that technology was a tool that would give him better visibility over what was happening at the company. So less than two years after he got his first computer, he decided to implement enterprise resource planning (ERP) using BAAN software. This is the integrated and electronic management of core-business processes. It gives companies one source of the truth rather than multiple, disjointed ones spread over different departments.

Many companies have rolled it out, but few have probably revolutionized their operations quite as fast as THP. The project director who came to implement ERP had previously worked for Carlsberg. She said it was like going from a bike to an airplane in one fell swoop, missing out on the motorbike and the car in between. The solution we chose cost $3 million, so it was another huge investment for us and difficult to know whether it was the right time for it.

We first implemented ERP in 2002, then upgraded it in 2006, and again in 2011 to SAP. Each time we wanted to make sure we got advice from the best and chose an internationally reputed implementation company to guide us through the process. However, shortly after our last upgrade, our CFO started to notice some odd numbers cropping up. On further investigation, we uncovered a whole raft of problematic areas.

It turned out that the internal ERP implementation team had been bypassing the steering committee and asking the external implementation company to make certain changes without anyone else's knowledge. These changes enabled the people involved to defraud the company—or perhaps I should say *continue* defrauding the company.

It was a very worrying time for the family, and we felt under personal threat. My brother Dũng woke up one morning to discover that his laptop had been taken from next to his bed, but not his wallet full of cash. It was a chilling message from the perpetrators. They wanted to show us that they could harm us if they chose to if we did not back off from our investigation.

But we did not back down, and they were fired as we progressively cleaned up the mess and restructured our IT governance and controls. We refused to make the balloon payment to the external implementation company and hired Deloitte to check whether there were other areas we had not been able to identify.

It was a difficult learning process, and it cost us a lot of money to clean up the mess, but there was one happy outcome. In the run-up to our THP Anniversary Day that year, our marketing team and external agency decided to make a short movie as a present for my father.

It was filmed as a kind of highly stylized, old-time Saigon noir; a thriller about the fraud called *The Super Five*, starring my father, mother, brother, sister, and me. It was great fun to make and a very cathartic way to put the fraud behind us.

The fact is that if SAP is implemented properly, the stringent controls embedded in the system processes make it very hard for fraud to occur in the first place. So, it is well worth the investment.

The best advice for any company considering such a big overhaul is to check references very carefully. Then put in lots of checks and balances, and do not try to rush the implementation. Computerization is one area where it does not pay to cut corners. It represents a once-in-a-lifetime transition for companies when they reach a certain size. It is critical to make it watertight.

> *Computerization is one area where it does not pay to cut corners. It represents a once-in-a-lifetime transition for companies when they reach a certain size. It is critical to make it watertight.*

It is also important to make sure you have a backup plan if the IT systems fail. Once THP had all the right systems in place, my father wanted to make sure the company could continue to function if they went wrong. Every year he runs disaster-management scenarios and stress tests the IT systems.

When Is a Shop Not a Shop?

Sales is another big area my father is always keen to have visibility over. Until the early 2010s, no one really knew what the department was up to, or whether they were selling what they said where they said. We counteracted this oversight by implementing a distribution management system (DMS), becoming the first Vietnamese company to do so.

This system has vastly improved our logistics and market intelligence (MI). It has made it far easier to detect patterns and improve efficiency. All our sales invoices are now put into this system.

It also helps us to manage our inventory better. As a rule of thumb, it gets prohibitively expensive to maintain inventory cover above the 90 percent mark. THP does not do this, but we do try to maintain 100 percent inventory cover for our most popular brands. It is always a work in progress. But it is unusual for us to get caught short on key lines.

My father has a massive dashboard in his office where he can monitor what is being delivered and where on a daily basis. Trucks have GPS trackers. We even upload photos of the smallest shop onto the DMS. This not only helps us check whether the signage and advertising are correct but also whether the shop even exists.

He soon realized that a number of the photos were fakes, and about a year after we implemented the DMS, we hired seventy investigators to audit the sales team. For every fraud they uncovered, we promised to pay them 50 percent of the penalty we imposed.

Within one month, they had uncovered three hundred thousand misrepresentations by various members of the sales team. The responsible person was fined the equivalent of about $10 per fraud. Some team members ended up having to repay two to three months' salary.

By the second month, the number of frauds had dropped to 30,000, then 2,500 by month three, and only 300 by month four. By this time, none of the original sales team was left. They had either resigned or been fired.

This 100 percent turnover rate was replicated twice over before we finally found a team that understood crime does not pay. My father likes to quote a famous Asian proverb: "Sometimes you have to kill the chicken to scare the monkey."

Reinforcing the Foundations

One of my father's other great skills is his ability to plan for the very long-term future and then put the processes in places to help him get there. Shortly after we hired Deloitte to sort out the SAP/ERP mess, we also hired AT Kearney to conduct an in-depth review of all our processes and help us set the stage to become a much bigger company.

At that point, we were experiencing linear growth. We wanted it to become exponential. AT Kearney gave us a road map to achieve it, but what we did not quite grasp immediately is that the map did not state how long the journey time should take.

We had restructured many processes, but there was no time limit on when they needed to be completed. This enabled some staff members to carry on being inefficient for twice as long as they were before. Managers were also saying they needed two to three times longer than they really did, so they would never be late completing a task.

The Vietnamese are not a naturally process-driven people. They find their own way of doing things. One look at the traffic in major cities convinces most visitors that the country thrives on organized chaos.

On the plus side, the Vietnamese are an inventive, creative people. Recent history has accentuated that. During the war, people resorted to making weapons from bamboo. After the war, import restrictions led my father to build his business from scrap parts. We are very good at making do with what we don't have.

In 2017, my father decided it was time to completely overhaul all the processes again and set proper time limits for each one. He sat down for three months and personally went through around two thousand processes and up to eight thousand work instructions and job descriptions. He made every department review their processes, and he took a hard line with anyone who did not embrace the project with the same dedication that he did.

One department head told my father it would take three months to go through thirty-five processes. He gave him ten days. The department head said it was not possible. On the first day, he and his team were assigned six processes, but their review did not meet my father's satisfaction. He told them they could not leave until he was happy. They finally left the office at three o'clock in the morning.

A few hours later, they were back at their desks again and had another six processes to get through. That day they were out by eight o'clock at night. On the third day, the senior managers left for the weekend and my father sat down with the junior staff himself. He helped them review eight processes. They were done by six o'clock.

When the senior managers returned on Monday, my father told them what had happened.

"You don't have incapable staff," he told them, "but I do seem to have incapable managers." It was just the call to action they needed. By day ten, all thirty-five processes had been reviewed.

Each staff member at THP now has a daily work plan with a list of priorities. Each of the company's processes have a lead time and a paid time—that is, staff get paid for the amount of time it should take to do a process and no more. If a process is not completed on time, the staff member in question is issued with a corrective-action request.

We assign an owner to each process to try to mitigate the temptation for one employee to ask a friend to overlook any delays and not issue a corrective-action request. If the process is late, the process owner is held responsible. It makes them far more attuned to what is happening right down the line.

We also ask people to view corrective-action requests in a different light. It is not a punishment for a work colleague they like but a means to help that person do his or her job better the next time.

The desire to be more effective stretches right up the management chain. One of the most important transitions we have made has been at the board level. In the past, my mother and father not only owned the company but made all the decisions as well. There was no channel to question their actions.

Creating a proper board of directors enabled us to create a structured conversation to enhance the company's decision-making. We wrote a board charter, established a meeting schedule, and created a few sub-board committees. I now chair our corporate social responsibility (CSR) committee, while my father oversees the remuneration committee.

This move coincided with the government's push to encourage better board-governance practices. Vietnamese companies are now required to have at least one independent board member.

We recognized the value of this, too, and our deputy chairman is now David Riddle, who is also our managing director of logistics bureau international. He also heads one of three subcommittees we created overseeing governance, audit, and risk with Peter Davies, our head of internal audit.

We have been building up our internal-audit function since 2015. It is something a lot of Vietnamese companies either do not have or pay lip service to. But we take it very seriously.

David and Peter are completely independent of my father and there are no limitations on what they can investigate. Their work has helped to vastly increase transparency at the company.

For example, we discovered that while some staff members were ticking all the right boxes, they were doing it out of sequence, so the process was not actually being followed even though it appeared to be on paper. In one instance, warehouse staff had been issuing "goods received notes" completely on trust before the goods actually arrived from our suppliers, or did not arrive in many instances.

One of the other areas AT Kearney advised us on was how to reorganize our overall company structure. This led to the establishment of several new divisions such as an export arm and a concentrates arm. Before that, we did not control the end-to-end process of making beverages ourselves. Now that we also produce the concentrates that go into the beverages, we do.

Aside from making our processes more efficient, the overhaul has also freed up my father's time. It was getting very hard for him to sign off on every single aspect of the company. He needs the mental space to do what he does best and come up with the overall strategy and vision.

However, having spent the better part of this book explaining why multinationals become bogged down by processes and layers of middle management, we know how important it is to make sure we do not find ourselves heading down a similar route. It is a fine balance.

New layers of management can free up the founder's time, but if those managers start establishing their own power bases by hiring new staff and creating silos, the end result is counterproductive. Companies can also end up losing sight of the fact that they exist to serve the customer. They become far too focused on fine-tuning their processes.

We have spent one decade putting the right processes in place and digitizing the company. But the next decade will be about people. It will be about how we incentivize them and how they do so for each other.

CHAPTER 7

Motivate Employees and Foster Community Spirit

ONE INDIVIDUAL CAN CHANGE THE WORLD, but when a group of individuals work together, the impact is magnified for good or for ill. To be successful, most companies realize they need to think very carefully about how their employees interact with each other, with senior management, and with the organization's customers.

It is typically less of an issue for small companies. The founder or founders normally dominate the discourse, and it is much more about managing and understanding their own personality and trigger points. This topic will be explored in chapter 8.

But as companies get bigger, the way the founder's ethos and values percolate down the company becomes very important. For THP, this is represented by the seven core values that will be discussed in Appendix 2. Staff compensation is based on adhering to them. At its heart, THP is a behavioral-driven company and not just a profit-driven one.

Bigger companies also need to think about how to foster the same level of dedication in the employees as the founder and what structures to put in place to ensure staff members interact well with each other to achieve it. In the West, great emphasis is placed on the word "teamwork." But this has tended to be an alien concept in Vietnam and throughout much of Asia.

It is something many multinationals struggle with when they try to import Western business practices to the region. This chapter will explore why Asian values are different to Western ones and how successful companies can take the best elements from each to drive their businesses and employees forward.

It will also discuss how THP tries to incentivize and empower its employees to do their personal best, both from a financial and operational standpoint. It also examines how a company's CSR (corporate social responsibility) program can not only help to embed it within the local community but also give its employees a greater sense of purpose and belonging.

Let East Be East, But Learn from West

One of the biggest mistakes Western companies make when they come to Vietnam is to try instilling a sense of teamwork. They will almost certainly fail. Teamwork is not one of THP's core values, for example.

We try to achieve the same outcome, but we wrap the concept up in very different language, which appeals to the Vietnamese mind-set. For example, we call our fifth core value "Owning your work."

This core value is about taking responsibility. Understand that success or failure is due to personal effort. Do not blame external factors for mistakes or take someone else's credit. Above all else, learn that helping others to achieve success equates to personal success as well.

This latter point tends to resonate the most with competitive type-A personalities who are typically self-focused as they clamber up the greasy pole. Once they get into management positions, they are often very ineffective until they realize they are being judged on their ability to support others. They start making an effort once they understand that making others look good makes them look good, too.

The Vietnamese find teamwork particularly difficult, because we are such a self-reliant people. History has made it so. Put too much trust and reliance in other people, and you will end up being subjugated by them.

The plus side of this self-reliance is that Vietnamese are very entrepreneurial. Most people have their day job and their small business on the side. Walk down the street, and you will see that nearly every house will have been turned into some small business or other.

Some of the country's bigger employers worry that this is affecting productivity. How can employees give a company 100 percent of their time and energy if they are busy working out how to grow their own small business, as well?

But this is not something we are overly concerned about at THP. One thing that any small businessman or woman soon learns is how hard it is to make money—or keep making it. People who have only ever been salaried employees do not have the same understanding of just how much effort is needed to generate enough revenue to pay the bills.

The second reason teamwork is such an alien concept for the Vietnamese relates to issues around face and respect. Asians are renowned for not wanting to lose face and for their attachment to hierarchy. Everyone needs to understand what someone else's status is.

This concept even embraces the family. No one ever says "sister" or "brother." It must be "elder sister" or "younger sister"; "elder brother" or "younger brother."

In the corporate world, this manifests itself as a desire to respect those at a more senior level and receive respect from those at a lower one. This attitude is prevalent in Vietnam, although it is not as strongly rooted in the culture as it is in Japan, Korea, and to a lesser extent, China.

Respect is important to the Vietnamese, but not to the extent of slavishly following someone more senior for fear of otherwise making him or her look bad (loss of face). And again, there is a north and south divide. We have a saying that northern people are more likely to agree to your face but not in their heart. It is a part of the country where looking good or making a superior look good is more important than ensuring the right outcome.

On one level, this respect for rank means that junior people do not like to speak up in meetings. This can have negative consequences if the people responsible for executing a project know if it's impossible to do so based on the direction of someone who is more senior but also more detached and less informed about it.

Constructive Disagreement

At THP, we spend a lot of time explaining that Dr. Thanh is not interested in "yes" people. One of his favorite ripostes is telling people that, "If you agree with me all the time, then one of us is unnecessary."

He wants people to respect his vision but to also express their opinions if they feel there is a better way to execute it. Asian educational systems do not tend to promote this kind of original thinking, so it is something we have to emphasize time and time again in our training sessions.

My sister, Bích, is currently our head of corporate service and governance. She spends a lot of time training managers and their teams on how to contribute ideas or contrary opinions without causing someone to lose face. Part of it comes down to showing they have actively listened to the person they disagree with. That is a sign of respect.

Part of it is about the tone of voice used to frame a different solution. This is also a sign of respect. For example, "I respect your vision, but I feel there is a different way we can execute this project."

It is also very important that the most senior managers lead by personal example. It is important for them to listen and understand what their more junior employees are thinking. So, we run meetings differently to most companies. We expect the most junior members of the team to put forward their points of view first, then the manager will frame a solution after listening to everyone.

Employees all over the world are also more motivated if they feel they are working for something bigger than themselves. If someone has a sense of belonging, he or she is not only far more likely to go the extra mile but also work with others to achieve it. This attribute is particularly strong in the Vietnamese, again thanks to the country's history.

The need to get rid of colonial oppressors forged a sense of unity. The Vietnamese people understand the negative consequences of conflict. They like to strive for a cause but one that makes them feel better about themselves. We encourage this at THP in all sorts of ways. One of the more lighthearted ones is our annual songwriting day.

Each year, we hold a songwriting competition and all the entrants are invited to our headquarters to take part in a gala performance. Some of the entries are by individual people, but most of them are by departments. They work on a song and routine together. They typically dress the same, as well.

They behave as a collective, but they still would not describe their actions as teamwork. What they have is a shared sense of ownership. Everyone feels they have a stake in the outcome and they take great pride in being able to showcase their work to their colleagues and the rest of the organization.

How Vietnam is moving up the economic value chain: leaders are trained not born.

Life Lessons

On a day-to-day level, it is also important to let people take risks and fail without undue consequences. Failure scares most people. They generally do not want to advertise their mistakes in case a rival uses the information against them.

We try to encourage THP employees to understand that failure is all around us, and there is no reason to be afraid of it. It is something we should respect and try to learn from.

Failure does not necessarily mean someone cannot do his or her job. For example, in the R&D section of the company, failure is generally a prerequisite before a breakthrough is made. It is the breeding ground for innovation.

Likewise, human beings often pretend they know more than they actually do. My father has very little time for this; he believes one person probably knows 1 percent, realizes he or she does not know another 2 percent, but is not aware there's a remaining 97 percent yet to grasp.

As a result, he constantly strives to better himself and his understanding of the world. He is not afraid to say he does not understand something, because he hopes someone else will be able to enlighten him.

Why? is one of his favorite questions, and when someone gives him an answer, he tends to ask it again a number of times until he feels he has the complete picture.

It is a rare personality trait. All too often, it feels like CEOs stick to the high-level discussion at annual general meetings in the hope that no one will press them on the fine detail they are probably unaware of. By contrast, my father believes true leaders are not afraid to reveal their vulnerabilities. This makes them stronger, not weaker.

This also means he is quite happy to accept challenges from very junior members of staff, or to answer what might seem like basic questions from them. This enables him to teach them and to carry on learning himself.

At THP, we also try to promote open communication and do not believe in hoarding information. Clearly, THP has a strategy, which it wants to keep confidential for competitive reasons. But as a family we are a big believer in self-improvement through learning. We want to pass on that knowledge to others.

In fact, my father likes training so much that it is what he wants to do when he retires: teach business management based on lessons learned from his own successes and failures. It is something he has always valued, right from the start. In the beginning, there were only three university-educated people at THP: himself, his wife, and Uncle Tu. Training was something the company needed.

One of the greatest perks THP offers employees is the opportunity to carry on learning. The Vietnamese educational system does not produce employees who are equipped for the workplace. It is a common problem across the world, and it means coaching or on-the-job training is very important. This is particularly the case in Vietnam where very few companies give their staff management or leadership training.

At THP, we do not mind if staff members take our training and leave, because that benefits society, too. My father loves nothing more than when former employees get in touch with him, or give him flowers on Teachers Day, which is celebrated on November 20 in Vietnam. It also helps to highlight THP's culture to other companies.

As a family, we believe in developing our capabilities so we can live life to the fullest. We believe in giving service to others. Many of our training programs are geared around this concept. In 2018, we trained managers to believe in our fourth core value: nothing is impossible.

Rewarding Values as Well as Targets

At the end of the day, most people come to work because they need to earn a living. THP makes sure it stays competitive by benchmarking compensation against the top FMCG companies in Vietnam. Our guiding motif is not to pay the minimum but to be a company people aspire to work for.

We also take a different approach to how we determine an employee's compensation. That approach has also changed significantly over time. Before 2010, the company never really let anyone go unless they had committed a criminal act. If someone was underperforming, they would usually be moved somewhere else.

Our guiding motif is not to pay the minimum but to be a company people aspire to work for.

In the past when someone was sick, they did not have insurance or pension cover. This was something my mother attended to herself, calling the doctor if they were ill and giving them a lump sum when they retired. My father also gave houses to two employees who had served twenty years and risen to high-level positions after continuously improving their knowledge and growing with the company. These days all our employees now have health insurance coverage.

Where pay is concerned, we place a huge value on adhering to the company's seven core values. If a staff member financially benefits the company but not the customer, we consider this an act of misconduct.

We also do not believe in the practice of forced bell-curve ranking—identifying a small number of winners and losers at either end, with the bulk of employees in the middle. We want to encourage every individual to do his or her best.

Instead, we graph performance with financial targets/core competency on the Y-axis and THP's values on the X-axis. Both are important. If someone hits all financial targets but has a bad attitude, he or she will not score higher than someone who has not hit the targets but has a good attitude.

We also aim to make sure the assessments are as fair as possible by sourcing input from everyone an individual person deals with. Even the highest managers are subject to confidential 360-degree reviews from their staff.

But perhaps what really sets us apart from most Vietnamese companies is how much time we spend assessing staff and giving them feedback: fourteen days every six months. This amount of time may seem excessive, but we really want to drive home the message that performance is about working in accordance with THP's core values.

Bích's main focus is to make sure that managers based at our new factories understand this. Many of them will have never met my father before so his values will not come naturally to them.

Indeed, the whole idea of putting the customer first will seem like an alien concept to many given the way many Vietnamese companies operate. To make sure it does not stay that way, Bích has devised a seven-day management program around THP's guiding principles.

Once they have completed the course, managers will be evaluated at thirty- and ninety-day intervals. If they are not adhering to the core values, or passing them onto their staff by then, they will be asked to repeat the course until they do.

We have also been thinking about how we can reward staff members who really embrace the company's seven core values. Since these are the family's values too, we decided to recognize our best employees as members of a broader THP family.

In 2017, we launched a formal program called the THP Family Pool for employees at supervisor level and above. We're aiming to extend it to the whole company.

The main inclusion criteria include being honest, helpful, hardworking, and dedicated to serving the customer. In return, we consider a pool member's family part of the Trần family and will fund the health care of a spouse and the health care and education of all their children, including overseas schooling, if that is what they would like.

Where the wider company is concerned, we try to ensure everyone feels they belong. My mother has always been an expert at this. For Children's Day every June 1, she sends each employee's children a gift and personalized letter. She buys Mooncakes for everyone to celebrate the Mid-Autumn Festival. One time, she personally cooked three thousand pots of stewed pork.

More recently, Bích and I have tried to improve everyone's physical and mental well-being by launching fitness and yoga classes at our HQ building. Vietnamese people tend to be thin, so it has taken a long time for the idea of fitness to catch on. Our more Western-oriented staff members were the first to sign up, but gradually more people have joined in. Since 2015, THP has even been competing in Vietnam's Ironman events. In 2016, we fielded four teams that included Bích and myself.

This is another area where local and smaller businesses have an advantage over multinationals. The founders know their employees and have forged personal links with them. For instance, I care about the people on my team. I want to support them, and I also want to understand what is happening in their personal lives in case it affects their professional one, too.

Giving Back to the Community

Local businesses are also best placed to understand how, when, and where to give back some of their profits to the local community. THP is a very strong believer in active corporate social responsibility (CSR), the acronym corporations have adopted for charitable giving.

Our third core value is to be a responsible member of Vietnamese community and society.

The company does not have a fixed CSR budget, nor does it allocate a set percentage of revenues. However, we are open to all suggestions and proposals that meet our criteria. Specifically, we want to improve the lives of young people, particularly in rural areas. We also target long-term development.

The company's charitable ethos comes from my maternal grandmother, Nguyen Thi Roan. When she was alive, she was constantly asking my mother for money. This made my mother worry, particularly as my grandmother would often try to get the family to eat rotten food.

However, my grandmother did that for a reason: so we could understand what it was like to be poor. When she died, dozens of bicycle rickshaw drivers turned up to her funeral. It turns out she had been donating the money to them and their families.

Giving something back is the right thing to do. And there is nothing softheaded about it from a business perspective, either. It promotes profits. Customers increasingly consider a company's CSR practices when they make shopping decisions. It also embeds companies in the communities where they are selling their products.

CSR builds bridges to the community—*literally*, in THP's case. One of our main projects is the Bridge of Dreams Initiative, which was launched in 2016. So far, we have built eighteen bridges across the Mekong Delta. Each bridge is thirty to forty meters long and two and a half meters wide.

They are located in the Mekong Delta, which is famed for its beautiful landscape, crisscrossed by rivers and small canals. However, this network isolates villages from the road transport system, making life difficult for villagers who cannot afford to build the bridges themselves.

The company has also been very active providing clean water, a natural resource we rely very heavily on for our drink products. We partner with community groups across the Mekong Delta to donate water-filtering equipment to convert briny water into potable water for drinking and cooking.

THP also has a program called the Golden Cattle program, which identifies needy families in poor provinces and awards them a pair of breeding cows. As of this writing, the company has donated three thousand cows since 2013. One of the driving philosophies behind THP's CSR programs is to foster self-sufficiency and independence.

Our CSR strategy is continually evolving. Sustainability also means being responsive in a timely manner. Responding to natural disasters is one way to do this. Thus, in 2012, THP changed one key aspect of the Anniversary Day celebrations.

Sports sponsorship Vietnamese style: the annual cow racing festival in the Seven Mountains Region of An Giang Province

Traditionally, all the guests would bring expensive flower baskets. However, in 2012 there were devastating floods across central and southern provinces. THP employees organized donations that generated over VND700 million for relief instead. This annual fundraising initiative is something we have continued ever since.

Another major way local companies set themselves apart is the events they sponsor. Multinationals tend to go for the big international sporting fixtures such as a country's grand prix. Local companies often have far better insight into national- or regional-level events with far greater resonance among the local population. It is a great exercise in brand-building.

For example, in 2008, THP set up and sponsored the first and only Vietnamese team to conquer Mount Everest. A national flag and a flag bearing "Number 1" were planted at the top.

> *In 2008, THP set up and sponsored the first and only Vietnamese team to conquer Mount Everest. A national flag and a flag bearing "Number 1" were planted at the top.*

Another local event that THP has been sponsoring since the turn of the century is cow racing in An Giang Province in the Mekong Delta. Each year on the final day of the Khmer calendar, the local Khmer population (one of Vietnam's ethnic minorities) holds a festival to honor their ancestors. The cow race, which takes place at the foot of the Ta Pa Mountain, is the highlight.

The racetrack, set in a muddy and slippery paddy field, is 120 meters long. Each race involves two pairs of cows, controlled by one or two men. The races are both exciting and hilarious. They are part rodeo, part race, and part comedy since cows are not renowned for their sprinting ability.

CHAPTER 8

Take Responsibility

THIS BOOK HAS TALKED a lot about yin and yang. Nowhere is this balancing of the two to create good boundaries (so one does not impinge on the other) more appropriate than in a discussion about work and life. It is particularly relevant for family-owned businesses where multiple members of the same family work together. The potential for broken boundaries and inter-marital, or inter-generational, conflict is practically limitless.

All human beings are a work in progress. We all make mistakes, and the Trần family is no different. This chapter will discuss how the family navigates these challenges and resolves family conflicts. One of the most important lessons we have taken onboard is that only by learning to manage ourselves can we hope to provide leadership for everyone else who works at THP and everyone who handles some of the crises that beset the company.

Vietnamese readers will already be very familiar with one unfortunate incident that happened a few years ago when a customer alleged he had found a fly in one of our drinks. The subsequent official investigation determined it was blackmail, but it created a lot of bad publicity and was a very trying time. But as this chapter will go on to explain, we took responsibility and have emerged on the other side a stronger company.

What Is Family?

It seems like such a simple question, but it can be surprisingly difficult to answer. Naming each member is the easy part. Explaining how they should all interact with each other is much harder. Should a family be governed like a nation with a constitution, or a company with its core values, principles, and charter?

Our family has its own mission statement and a set of core values just like our company does (see Appendix 3). We regularly re-visit these values, discuss them at family meetings, and then refine them. We all agree to abide by them.

We have found them an indispensable checklist. They bound us together at a time when we were fraying at the seams. They have helped keep us close knit and made our working life far more straightforward.

Part of the thanks should go to the Landmark Forum, a US-based organization specializing in professional and leadership development. My father first hired them back in 2009 to help coach senior managers of the company.

He is a firm believer that leaders are trained, not born, and he wanted to build a sustainable organization that had integrity, was customer focused, and whose employees worked well together. He did not want one where the head told the legs to walk, but one where they either stood still, or delayed setting off.

The training proved incredibly worthwhile in terms of building a culture of integrity that has underpinned THP's growth and sustainability. Today there is an ambassador representing each of THP's core values in every single department.

My father also soon decided it would make a lot of sense for Landmark to help "transform the family" as well. We should be the foundation stone for developing leaders across the company. Family-owned businesses only work well when there is good communication between different family members and across the generations.

At that point in time, THP had been expanding at a rapid clip for more than a decade. The demands that growth was producing had started to nip at the edges of family solidarity. Both Bích and I had also finished university and returned to Vietnam to work for THP.

The family coaching we did was an eye-opening experience for all of us. One of the most important things we learned was how to listen to someone fully and be generous, so we gave another person the space to express an opinion without butting in or mentally preparing our own retort. We learned how to free other family members from our prejudices about who they were and what they were capable of, and to give them space to be the best people they could be. Our parents also had to learn to view Bích, Dũng, and me as adults and not young children they needed to take care of.

It took us six months to complete the practical aspects of the program—and it was tough. The whole exercise lasted a year and a half. But it gave us valuable new ways of communicating with each other. By forming new patterns of behavior, we were able to carve out a different and more positive future for the family. We continue practicing its methods to this day.

Unsurprisingly, we learned to understand each other much better over that period of time. For one thing, Bích and I finally grasped why our parents behaved in ways which had not made us happy as children. Until then, I was never even sure my father loved the rest of the family.

I was always so frightened of him as a child. He seemed so stern and unforgiving. He once thrashed me so badly I was physically sick. One time, Bích wet herself after he walloped her for playing on top of an employee's car. My father did it because he wanted us to respect THP's employees. To understand that they were the ones generating the income that put rice on our table. Not to think of ourselves as the center of the universe, but learn to serve others rather than expect to be served ourselves.

He did not want us to grow up as the entitled children of rich parents and was forever bringing us back down to earth if he thought we were giving ourselves airs and graces. I did not fully comprehend this at the time. I just thought it was not fair that other children had toys, whereas I had to make my own from scraps on the factory floor.

As chapter 3 explained, my father spent much of his childhood at the orphanage being flogged for some perceived misdemeanor or other. It made him a stronger person and he thought it would help us too. One of his favorite sayings to our mother was, "We're bringing up children not chickens. They have to learn to stand on their own two feet."

But the personal development work we did also helped my father to understand himself and how his childhood experiences had made him the person he was. He understood that just because certain experiences had shaped him, they were not necessarily the best ones to apply to others. Someone who is successful in life often attributes his or her achievement to certain traits picked up in childhood and then tries to replicate them ad infinitum. But that is not always the best method. One of the most difficult aspects of the training was defining the inner self. For most people it is even harder than defining what a family should stand for. What we learned is that people have very different ways of doing this.

Some people never get beyond their senses. They live to eat, or drink, or shop. These people are living organisms, ones that live and die without ever really knowing who they are or why they exist. For some, the family is all-important. For others it is an organization. For others still it is the nation. Ho Chi Minh is a very good example of someone who put the idea of nation above all others. Martin Luther King and Gandhi are others.

For Bích, the answer is an organization: THP. A few years ago, she told my father to think about all the employees and their families after he broke down when my mother had a stroke and was then diagnosed with cancer. He was not sure he could carry on if something happened to her. My sister told him that she also felt despair, but he could not give up just because he felt like it. She told him he had to put the company and its employees first.

Once a person has a true sense of self, he or she then must learn how to manage it. This is one of the things human beings tend to find most difficult in life. People are generally prone to go far easier on themselves than others. It is much easier to shift the blame elsewhere than to understand how we may have been at fault.

But how can people manage or lead others if they cannot manage themselves? In this context, taking responsibility does not mean taking control of a situation and issuing instructions to make ourselves feel good about our superior status or the power we wield over others. It means understanding our own personality and how that affects other people.

The Generation Game

The psychological work our family did really helped us to deeply understand the responsibility we have to each other and ultimately to THP as well, for responsibility is one of the key requirements for sustaining a business from one generation to the next.

There is a Vietnamese proverb that says, "The rich do not stay rich and the poor do not stay poor for three generations." It underscores the challenges of making sure the second generation stays as motivated as the first when they no longer have financial hardship to spur them on.

Not for nothing does a variant of that proverb suggest that the first generation makes the money, the second generation spends it, and the third generation blows it. From rice paddy back to rice paddy again; the wheel comes full circle.

Much has been written about the best way for family business owners to transfer that sense of responsibility to the next generation. My father has been quoted on CNBC on this question saying, "I have to choose the right person to become the CEO of the company and give this responsibility to the most competent individual. I hope my children will work hard to achieve that distinction, instead of automatically assuming they'll be given the position, because inheriting a business is not a privilege, but a responsibility."

> *My father may have been very harsh when we were growing up, but he wanted to create a culture of hard work where merit is rewarded. As a result, my sister and I both work as hard as he does.*

My father may have been very harsh when we were growing up, but he wanted to create a culture of hard work where merit is rewarded. As a result, my sister and I both work as hard as he does. In fact, these days we get less sleep than he does, as we only sleep for four hours, and he has switched from four to six. He has also started going to the gym six days a week. He is someone who never does anything in half measures.

When he used to sleep for only four hours, he would frequently want to run ideas past us at all times of the day or night. Because we all lived "above the shop," he always knew where we were. Sometimes I would have to beg him to let me sleep. In this instance, the boundaries between work and home were not so strong.

When the company was first established, there were no boundaries at all. We literally lived in the factory. My father's office was also the family living room.

These days we live in an apartment above the factory and try to eat together twice a day. This is when we swap information and ideas. No one tries to hoard information. It keeps the lines of communication open and strong.

But when we are at work, we only refer to each other as Dr. Thanh, Madam Nụ, Miss Bích and Miss Phương. It is how we try to maintain good boundaries and make them clear to all our colleagues.

For example, in the workplace, I need to respect my father as my boss, but he also needs to respect my professional opinion even if it differs from his. He talks to me as a valued colleague and supervisor, not as a father talking to a daughter.

In turn, I also must take responsibility for my mistakes as anyone else at THP does. But it has not always been like this. There was a time when my father would scold me, and my mother would get upset with him for doing so.

She did it out of love for me, but it did not help me to learn from my mistakes. I asked her to let me handle things by myself, and to her credit she stepped back from the situation and did not involve herself in these types of incidents in the future. After all, I needed to gain the trust of my boss just like any other employee.

My father also learned that he needed to pay me a salary when I first joined THP. It was something he had not even thought of. But I successfully argued that I needed to hold myself accountable for the work I had completed, and a salary would reflect my performance. I won the argument, and both my brother and sister were paid when they joined in later years.

We recently held a one-day event for suppliers, and one of the main questions that kept coming up was how to manage multi-generational family businesses. Many of our suppliers have similar backgrounds to ours. They were founded around the same time in Vietnam's history and have grown alongside us. They are still run by the original founders working alongside their children. One of their main concerns is how to avoid spoiling the next generation, which is growing up against the backdrop of a much richer country.

What we said is that most successful multi-generational family businesses take very specific steps to transfer family values from one generation to the next. These include:

1. **Expectation of Achievement and Rejection of Entitlement**. Younger members need clear standards for behavior and achievement. Joining the family business should not be viewed as an automatic right. It is something which should be earned, not inherited.

2. **Respect for Elders**. Respect for elders is a very Asian value, but it is key to success in any culture. After all, the senior

members take responsibility for setting the "tone at the top." All corporate cultures start from the top.

3. **Understanding the Second Generation**. Second-generation individuals will have grown up in different circumstances, so it is important that the first generation understands what motivates them.

4. **Respect for Stories**. This is how successful companies communicate their core values and mission. It helps all family members to understand and remember what makes their family unique.

The stories require inter-generational conversations. Most of these conversations are informal, happening over dinner and casual meetings. But formal conversations can also work. Some families schedule time, or a formal meeting, every month or every quarter so that family members can sit together and have conversations that span all generations.

Sometimes having a facilitator makes these conversations more productive. Structures are put in place for elders to speak to all and roles are established for mentors and coaches within the family. Establishing family activities is also good, as it helps to enhance family values.

Accountability Starts with Self

As I said earlier in the chapter, it is all too easy to shift the blame when something goes wrong. It was down to a competitor, a customer, faulty products, irresponsible employees, suppliers, or the general economy, etc. It is always easier to find excuses and far harder to embrace setbacks and mistakes with the same enthusiasm as triumphs and victories. It is human nature.

And yet, true leadership means taking responsibility for failure as well as success. The two go hand in hand. Only when someone accepts there is no one else to blame, then and only then can he or she develop a plan to succeed.

> *True leadership means taking responsibility for failure as well as success. The two go hand in hand. Only when someone accepts there is no one else to blame, then and only then can he or she develop a plan to succeed.*

Instead of asking, "Who did this to me?" the question should be reframed as, "What did I do wrong?" This becomes the far more constructive self-help. As the saying goes, "It never gets easier, you get better."

It is a difficult truth. But taking ownership means accepting that you are the source of the problem. You are the only thing you can change or control. So, if there is a difficulty, own it. Never blame anyone else. Have confidence that by changing yourself, you can change the environment, too. Leaders who do this are far more likely to inspire the kind of loyalty and trust that makes companies succeed.

My father is a big advocate for John Maxwell's five levels of leadership. He is a big believer in level three: people not only follow someone because they want to (i.e., the relationship they have with them, which is classified as level-two leadership) but also because of their track record. This is when companies really start to produce results.

At THP, we try to empower all team members to act as if they are the owners of the enterprise, as well: to take responsibility for their successes and mistakes; to stay authentic and retain their integrity. If they stay true to what they believe and are open about what is working or not working, then they can successfully address problems, drive results, and improve performance.

Leaders and employees who can do this typically have an air of humility about them, which wins people over and inspires their loyalty. One good example of this kind of leadership in action comes from Emirsyah Satar, CEO of Indonesia's Garuda Airlines. Several times a year, he gathers his top leadership team to clean the company's airplanes.

He launched the initiative to remind his executive team that whatever important work they were doing, it was no more important than keeping Garuda airplanes clean and hygienic for their customers. No one was excused from taking part. Satar himself cleaned the toilets.

Staying humble and grounded becomes ever more difficult as people become more successful. They start to believe their own hype, a breeding ground for arrogance and the kind of hubris that leads to mistakes and a swift return to planet earth with a thump. The reality is that while THP became very successful during the early part of the century, much of that had to do with what was happening in Vietnam as a whole. The economy was on fire and all companies were doing well.

That is not to say my father would not have made a success of his life in different circumstances. He has the personality traits, which give him enormous drive. But he has always known that timing has played a big factor in his success as well. That and the hard work everyone puts into THP.

Nevertheless, we all got a wake-up call about accountability and staying humble in 2014 when we were accused of selling a drink with a fly in it. Being accused of selling adulterated products is just about the worst thing a fast-moving consumer-goods company can experience.

In this case, a man in Tien Giang Province claimed he had found a fly in a bottle of our Number 1 energy drink. He asked us for VND1 billion ($44,100) to pay for his silence. He subsequently reduced it to VND500 million ($22,050) but threatened to release his complaint to the newspapers and TV if we did not pay up. We set up a meeting with the man and handed over the VND500 million ($22,050). What he did not realize is that the police were already investigating the case and he was arrested in the act of receiving the money.

However, we did not win any plaudits for our actions. On the contrary, we soon found ourselves in the eye of a media storm. It whipped up very quickly and it continued for months. The words "THP" and "fly" quickly became the hottest ones across social media. The story gained a life of its own.

At one point, social-media users speculated that my father had a nineteen-year-old mistress who was running the factory into the ground. There was even a suggestion that one employee had died after falling into a production tank. Everyone believed there had been a fly in a Number 1 bottle.

And it did not just stop at online trolling. There was a Facebook page calling for a boycott of THP's products and organizing demonstrations against the company. It cost us dearly in terms of value—VND2 trillion—not to mention the fact that it costs about six to seven times more to acquire a new customer than it does to retain one.

The court ruled in our favor and our accuser was sent to prison. There were signs of tampering with the bottle. The water level was also lower. The Ministry of Public Security's Criminal Science Institute investigated the case and found that the cap of the bottle had been punctured with a sharp object.

Still, from THP's perspective, the communications crisis was overwhelming. As the dust settled, we also concluded that the campaign against us had been orchestrated. Who stood to gain from our loss of market share?

But one of the mistakes we made was appearing arrogant. Consumers did not like the fact that we had come down so hard on one man who had accused us of negligence. The public perception was that we did not seem to be playing fair with consumers, even though one of them had not played fair with us. It was a very valuable business lesson. Even if others do not play fair and adopt dirty tactics, we must still handle it correctly ourselves, for at the end of the day, any one person's perception is their own truth.

My father has always said that the most important thing we must do is listen to the consumers. They are not always right, as the saying goes, but their voice is powerful, and we should always be listening.

In Vietnam there is a famous saying, "Tiếng chào cao hơn mâm cỗ." It literally means, "A greeting is more important than a tray of banquet food." In other words, the way I invite you to my party is more important than what I serve you. We had forgotten this truism.

But the Vietnamese are a tolerant people, again thanks to a history of managing conflicts. If someone acknowledges that they have acted wrongly and shows genuine empathy, then they will be forgiven. My father took this to heart and personally led our "sorry" campaign.

He wanted people to know that he understood he should have handled the situation better. He also has his own saying: "All storms are sudden, unpredictable, and cause damage. But once the storm recedes, the grass and trees will blossom and thrive."

And that was the case in this instance. Since then, we have tried to be much more open as a family. We realized that people knew THP well, but they did not know the family behind it. We want to show them that we are essentially no different from anyone else. We have our own strengths and weaknesses. This book is one result of that attempt to connect.

We have also opened the factory to visitors so they can see our production standards firsthand. And then there is social media. We learned a lot about the harm it can bring, but now we are harnessing it to reach out and communicate with our customers directly. My father's personal website and advice column are the direct result of it.

Part III:
A Woman's World

For the first time in Vietnam's history, every woman is gaining the opportunity to pursue her dreams, whether as a career woman, a stay-at-home mother, or someone who tries to juggle both. Companies that want to be successful need to understand what makes women tick, as we are an equal part of the country's workforce in terms of numbers, if not yet in terms of pay or prestige.

Mine is the generation where many young middle-class women have grown up in Vietnam and then studied abroad—or who have grown up abroad and then returned to Vietnam. There are few other countries around the world with such a large number of young people who feel so at ease in both worlds.

This perspective has given us a global and local mind-set, which is turning out to be a huge advantage for the country. It is also helping women to throw off some of the shackles history has heaped on us faster than other countries in the region.

I, for example, am someone who will always be Vietnamese in my heart, but these days I feel equally at home wherever I am in the world. And in this final part of the book, I would like to share my own personal story, exploring the influences which have shaped my life and the wider role women play in Vietnamese society. I hope it helps other young women to understand that there is no gender bias to "nothing is impossible."

My sister and I both know we are very privileged to be the stewards for the second generation of the Trần family at THP. We are emblematic of a shift that is taking place at family-owned businesses across Asia. These days it is often not just a generational transition but a gendered one as well. We have spent much of this book discussing how local companies can stand up to multinationals, but perhaps we also now need to find a new female name to replace David in the parable of the battle against Goliath.

CHAPTER 9

Globalized Girl

ONE OF THE DEFINING EVENTS of my childhood was the day my maternal grandmother found me on the floor dirty, unattended, and chasing after a mouse I was hoping to eat because I was so hungry. Another was the day she found me after I fell off a cupboard, screaming with pain after slicing my finger open. I still bear the scars today.

These two incidents convinced my grandparents that I should live with them. My parents were all consumed with work, and at that point we did not have the money for childcare.

But it is unlikely my father would have agreed to pay for it even if he could have afforded to. He is not a miserly man, but as I have said many times throughout this book, he is one who believes in self-reliance—even for young children. He was very keen that we did not become what he calls, "attached to the universe like an umbilical cord."

He was forever telling my mother that it would do us no good if we were cosseted and overprotected. "No one serves you. You have to serve yourselves and serve others." That was his refrain. Even after THP started making money, he would tell us that he planned to give it all away to charity. He wanted us to stand on our own two feet as he had done.

I was about three years old when I went to live with my grandparents. My parents continued to play a big role, as they laid down the rules and were very strict. While I lived with my grandparents, though, mine was a very sheltered life, filled with books and reading. Every day my grandfather, Pham Van Vat, took me to school on his bicycle. I was not allowed to walk there like most of the other students.

My grandmother and I were also very close, right up until the day she died in 2002. Her influence and moral code would have a lasting and positive impact on my life. Hers was not an easy life. Two of her children died because of Vietnam's upheavals. Another fled abroad. She dedicated her life to helping others.

By the time I returned to my parents, I was ten years old and my sister Bích and brother Dũng had come on the scene. My sister and I fought quite a lot during our childhood, while I became something of a mother figure to Dũng. But I did not understand what nurture meant then. If he did something wrong, I would beat him with a stick.

I thought discipline was the key—as I had learned from my father. Then one day, I suddenly thought, *Why am I doing this? Is it because he has done something wrong and should be punished, or is it because it makes me feel good to be in control?* From that moment on, I stopped. I was about twelve and he would have been seven.

Our family life was part and parcel of the factory. There was no distinction between the two, and meals were spent discussing THP business. But we were not yet encouraged to voice our opinions. In Vietnam, parents expect children to be seen and not heard, just like Western ones a century ago. But my sister, brother, and I were like sponges soaking up the information, and our father was happy to instruct us.

Both our parents have always been very focused on value. They have no interest in buying fancy cars or clothes. They showed us that the path to success is to invest every resource into the family business, mentally and financially.

When it comes to money, I am a natural saver too. That desire was there from the beginning, part of my genetic makeup. For example, my grandmother gave me lunch money, but I always tried to save as much as possible. My grandfather opened an account for me with a local bank so I could watch my savings grow.

> Both our parents have always been very focused on value. They have no interest in buying fancy cars or clothes. They showed us that the path to success is to invest every resource into the family business, mentally and financially.

Tết was a particularly exciting time of the year, as that is when I received lucky money known as "lì xì" in Vietnamese. Every lunar New Year, or Tết Nguyên Đán, adults wish children a happy year ahead by giving them red packets with lì xì inside.

Money has a special resonance in Asian culture. The New Year horoscopes always spend far more time explaining what someone's financial prospects are than their romantic ones. The color red also signifies good luck and prosperity. I would eagerly deposit my money into my savings account.

By the time I graduated from high school in 1999, I had saved $5,000. This was a considerable sum for a teenager—especially compared to the average annual income of just $1,850 in Ho Chi Minh City at that time. When I left university, I handed it to my father and asked him to invest it in the business.

As I entered my teenage years, I started to question my parents as most children of that age do. My father can be very stubborn and controlling, but he is also a very good listener, and if someone can marshal his or her arguments coherently, then he will generally agree. One of my biggest tests in this regard was where I should study.

I was very keen to go abroad. I really wanted to be exposed to new ideas and different points of view. I had also begun studying English and wanted to put those language skills to use. So, I had my eye on several universities in the US, Australia, and the United Kingdom.

But my father was very resistant. His general view on education is that "we study well because of our own efforts and not because of the school we go to. One school is the same as any other if we don't put in the effort."

He had even stronger views about studying abroad. "Overseas universities are for the ignorant and stupid because they want to escape school and are scared of failing the university entrance exam," he said. "Show me your results and then we can talk."

I was determined to prove him wrong and studied incredibly hard for the exam. I passed, and I still consider it one of the key milestones of my life. A month of further negotiation ensued before he eventually relented and said I could attend university in the US, if

I attended college for two years in Singapore first. Even with his own family, he drives an incredibly hard bargain.

My success paved the way for Bích to go to the UK and Dũng to the US when it was their turn. I took both of them, as my father was too busy, and it is an accepted part of Asian culture for the eldest sibling to take the lead.

My own time in Singapore was an eye-opener. Going there was daunting, as I had never spent a night outside the extended family home. But at the same time I was excited about the next stage of my life and the challenges it would bring. And I didn't forget the lessons my parents taught me.

There was one particular instance where I adopted my father's "nothing is impossible" attitude. It was in 2000, the start of a new millennium, and yet none of the students had individual access to the Internet. They either had to go to a shared service at the university or pay to use one of the new Internet cafes popping up across the city.

I really wanted my own line. The owner of the homestay where I was living was hostile to the idea and tried to make it difficult for me. But I persevered. I visited the post office and registered for an Internet service. I assembled all the necessary paperwork.

I was a mere college student, but I was aware that Singaporean bureaucrats follow rules to the letter. It can be very frustrating, but if residents know their way around the system, then they can often get what they want. Three days later I had functioning Internet in my room.

Studying and living in Singapore really opened my eyes. I noticed how people often thought differently from the way I did. I realized the world was a much bigger and infinitely more complicated place than I had imagined.

I was seeing globalization firsthand and for the first time. Singapore is a true *entrepôt* of people and international trade. I saw the opportunities it offered and realized there was so much to learn. I redoubled my studies to earn my degree. For my graduation thesis, I chose a project about Heineken, the Dutch-based beer company. The experience proved invaluable as I saw how one multinational develops projects and manages its brands close up.

In the meantime, I also had to earn some spare cash, so I took a job in a restaurant/bar as a promotional girl. My job was to welcome guests and encourage patrons to buy more beer. I worked from five o'clock to eleven o'clock at night.

There was a small fixed salary, but the bulk of my income came from commissions based on how much beer patrons purchased. I soon became adept at the art of being friendly without crossing boundaries—or creating expectations.

Being exposed to the Heineken organization made me wonder whether I should join a multinational or return home to THP. I was twenty-two years old and had to decide which path to take. Should I stay in Singapore and prepare myself for a career at a multinational? Or return to Vietnam?

I knew the big advantage of working outside the family business would be the ability to own my achievements and failures. Family relationships would not benefit or protect me. Any respect my colleagues showed me would be earned, not grudgingly bestowed because I was related to the owner. Moreover, by working in an established company, I would be able to compare and contrast the structures and operations of a developed organization with a family-owned one.

But there were also drawbacks. I knew I would have to work for quite a few years before I would realistically be given any kind of managerial responsibility. I also knew my career could be derailed at any time by corporate politics, mergers, bankruptcies, or other financial realities outside my control.

And then there was THP and my parents, to whom I wanted to prove so much. After a great deal of back and forth, my father told me I should make my own decision. He agreed that THP was not an easy company for any employee let alone a family member. He accepted that he could be a difficult boss.

Then he told me about an opportunity that would make a challenging but interesting entry point for me at THP. He was about to turn the company from a paper-based one to a digital one by implementing enterprise resource planning (ERP).

He said it would be a vet-the-business event and one that would expose me to every corner of the organization. I knew it would be years before I would have that kind of opportunity elsewhere. So, I accepted a job as an assistant to the marketing director.

Daddy's girl: striving to be a worthy successor

The next stage of my journey at THP had begun. Before I had lived there as a child, now I was one of the employees, later a manager, and today, a director in charge of communications and procurement. Since then, I have striven to be a worthy successor to my parents by learning how to be a manager, while living and teaching THP's core values. It is a work in progress.

My father always encourages his children to take risks so that we can learn from our mistakes. His view is that if I am not failing enough, then I am not taking enough risk. Another one of his favorite sayings runs thus: "When the boat sets out to sea, it is likely to encounter storms. The challenge is learning to control the boat when that storm comes."

My father remains a hard taskmaster and he is still apt to scold those he loves dearest, although he now has a much better understanding of why his childhood has made him thus. My father does not get angry very often, but on the few occasions when he does, I have learned how to stay calm and in control of the situation.

I find the most effective way to deal with the situation is to simply touch his arm. It brings him back into the present and reminds him that he is faced with another human being.

Getting defensive or fighting back does not work with him—and is generally not a good way to deal with anyone in life. As the famous saying goes, you cannot control other people, only your own reaction. So, I do not outwardly react. I simply ask what I can do to help.

With this response, people do not feel they have been backed into a corner, nor do they feel bad about their emotional outpouring and project that negativity back onto you. It really helps to defuse the situation and foster constructive agreement.

Many of the management techniques I have learned have resulted from my decision to join the Young Presidents' Organization (YPO), a global platform for chief executives to engage, learn, and share. Every CEO needs someone to turn to for insight and perspective, but there are generally only a limited number of people they can trust. Thanks to YPO, I can have confidential peer-to-peer conversations with other people like me.

YPO has really opened my eyes, because I have encountered many leaders who remind me of my father. It has given me some distance to understand his amazing talent and to see his limitations for the first time.

Even today, he is still constantly challenging me to test my abilities to the limit. He was at it again in 2017 when I decided to hold a one-day seminar for our suppliers, so we could share our knowledge of how family-owned businesses are run.

He wanted me to succeed, but he kept telling me I would fail—every single day. He also told me he would not be coming to the event. I asked him what I needed to do to change his mind.

He told me I needed to get five hundred people signed up. It was quite a tall order, since I was charging attendees a substantial registration fee to make sure we got the kind we wanted. But I did it—though not without some degree of anxiety as the deadline grew ever close. A number of suppliers even registered their entire family to attend.

Then, right before the event, my father told me he still would not be able to come because he had a sales meeting that clashed with it. I knew he was posturing to demonstrate that his time was valuable.

But he eventually rescheduled his meeting and came along as I believe he had always intended to beneath the hardened front. He just wanted me to prove that I could sign up five hundred people. The day itself was a great success, and we got a lot of positive feedback from other families wondering how to manage the succession from one generation to the next.

My father has always been my idol. One of the reasons I only sleep for four hours a night may be because I used to lay awake as a child wondering if he would come to my room and chat with me. I cherished those moments, and I can still hear the sound of his footsteps approaching in the depths of night. It has become an ingrained habit.

My father has always been my confidant. No one gives me better advice. And as I moved from my teenage years, he also really started to encourage me to voice my own opinions and develop cogent arguments. He was pleased when I did but challenged me when I did not.

He has never sought to impose his dreams on me. He has only ever followed his own and encouraged me to do the same.

I have never even felt pressured to get married or provide him with any grandchildren, which is very unusual in Asian culture. In fact, he has given me the freedom to choose who I want to be.

> *My father has also taught me that everyone is entitled to their own opinions—but not to their own facts. To this day, I feel fortunate to have this ongoing guidance, knowing that many children do not.*

My father has also taught me that everyone is entitled to their own opinions—but not to their own facts. To this day, I feel fortunate to have this ongoing guidance, knowing that many children do not. My father himself says he would like his own mentor, too, so he would not have to learn everything based on his own experience.

In recent years, our family has come under immense emotional strain because of my mother's health problems. It almost broke my father, but she showed us that she was the strong one. My mother has a very strong Catholic faith, and her view was that "whatever cross God has given me, I can bear." Her strength helped my father to discover his own.

It made the family realize that all the work my parents have done over the years was for each other. The Vietnamese are not a verbally demonstrative people. We do not tend to say we love each other. Love is demonstrated by our actions. For almost forty years my mother and father had lived and worked together, keeping their personal lives to a minimum and gradually forgetting themselves.

But this terrible time helped them to reconnect and understand what we were all working so hard for. That knowledge has made our family stronger. We believe we can overcome any crisis.

We all have to endure loss. The Vietnamese understand this only too well thanks to the events of the mid twentieth century. I am acutely aware that we only live once, so we need to make it count. One day my father will pass the baton to the next generation. I want to demonstrate I am living a life that counts. I hope I make him proud.

CHAPTER 10

#MeToo Vietnam

"IF WOMEN ARE NOT EMANCIPATED, socialism is only half-established." This was one of Ho Chi Minh's most famous quotes. It was very similar to Chairman Mao's dictum that "women hold up half the sky."

In Vietnam, the Workers Party of Vietnam (then known as the Communist Party of Vietnam from 1976) under Ho Chi Minh's leadership did a huge amount to uproot some of the most oppressive aspects of patriarchy during the middle of the twentieth century. Wife beating was publicly condemned, and child marriage was outlawed. Communists even enshrined female emancipation in the 1946 constitution: "Women enjoy equal rights with men in all spheres of life: political, economic, cultural, social, and familial."

However, come the twenty-first century, male dominance remains well entrenched in Vietnamese society. As this book was being written, the #MeToo movement erupted across the world after allegations about the sexual misconduct of American movie mogul Harvey Weinstein were reported by the *New York Times* and the *New Yorker*. Since then, scores of women in country after country across the world have shared their experiences of sexual harassment and gender inequality using the #MeToo hashtag.

In this chapter, I would like to explain how women's lives have changed in Vietnam, as well as share examples of the sexism I have experienced and what THP is doing to support women in the workplace. By discussing these sensitive and difficult issues, I hope it will lead to a better dialogue and working relationship between the sexes.

It is a particularly pertinent issue for local companies, or multinationals based in the Asian region, because it is an area of the world that still lags behind the west in terms of gender equality. Sexism in Vietnam does not seem to be as bad as in other parts of East Asia. The country's struggle for independence from colonial rule is partly to thank for that. However, sexism is still alive and kicking, as I have personally discovered a number of times.

> *Vietnam has a long history of having to stand up for itself, and women have played an active role in doing that. This has made Vietnamese women more emancipated than in other parts of the region.*

The historical dominance of China means that one of the many issues Vietnam has had to deal with is the Confucian view about a woman's role in society. When our northern neighbor invaded, Vietnam adopted the Confucian Three Obediences: "tại gia tòng phụ, xuất giá tòng phu, phu tử tòng tử." (A woman should obey her father as a daughter, her husband as a wife, and her sons in widowhood.)

But if this was the yin, then there was also a yang. Vietnam has a long history of having to stand up for itself, and women have played an active role in doing that. This has made Vietnamese women more emancipated than in other parts of the region. For example, two of the most famous figures in Vietnamese history are the Trưng sisters who led a peasant army against Chinese invaders during the first century AD and then proclaimed themselves as queens.

They were eventually defeated in battle, though no one quite knows how they died. One story has it that they jumped into a river and turned into statues, which washed ashore and were placed in Hanoi's Hai Bà Trưng Temple for worship. But their legend lives on, and many towns and villages across the country honor their sacrifice by naming streets and monuments after them.

More recently, the struggle for independence did a huge amount to change women's lives and their perceptions of the role they should play. North Vietnam built one of the largest contingents of women ever to fight in a war.

The resistance's official slogan was, "Let women replace men in all tasks in the rear." They ran supply lines, acted as spies, and made many of the rudimentary weapons from bamboo. But many fought and held those guns, too.

Those who did not fight also became used to not having men around and doing the jobs they would normally have done. My paternal grandmother was a case in point. Her first husband left home to join the Việt Minh, the League for the Independence of Vietnam, founded and led by the Vietnamese communists. She suddenly had to make all her own decisions and discovered she enjoyed it.

She was a strong woman, and when she later married my grand-father, she had no intention of living in his shadow. My grandfather had a building-materials business, and she decided to become the construction contractor: buying and leveling the land. She also built up a trucking business to support it. She was a natural businesswoman, but it caused conflict with her husband, and they eventually separated before her untimely death in a traffic accident.

My own mother is also a natural businesswoman and strong character, too. She came from a poor neighborhood and was determined to escape the fate of many of her contemporaries: getting married while still a teenager. In Vietnam, girls traditionally marked this rite of passage before the age of eighteen by painting their teeth black.

While she was at school, my mother made money by writing articles and publishing them in a weekly bulletin that she distributed to other classes. She also rejected the advances of one smitten young man from a wealthy family, because she valued her independence so much.

He had been secretly taking his parents' money to buy her clothes and gold rings. But she was not impressed and gave them back. She told him she did not like the fact he had not earned the money himself.

He got angry and told her that women who do not rely on their husbands have no worth. She retorted that the reverse was true. "In the future, I will be the one earning money for myself and you'll be the one depending on other people," she replied.

This incident convinced my mother to continue her studies, and after she completed high school, she entered university to study law. Sadly, her family's financial circumstances meant she had to leave before she could complete her degree. At that point, she started her sugar stall instead.

After she married my father, it was she who did the heavy lifting. He would produce the sugar, and she would be the one who carted it to market. Every day she had to carry more than a ton of sugar on her shoulders.

Iron ladies Nu, Phuong, and Bich: two generations of Tran women celebrating the successful completion of Vietnam's Ironman event, 2016

Later, she began trading sugar across the country. But what she really traded was sleep for work. She rarely slept for more than a few hours at night. One day she was so tired that she fell off her motorbike as she was driving past Bà Đen Mountain, close to the Cambodian border, en route to see a customer.

She was so tired that she just fell asleep in the ditch she had toppled into. She was greatly relieved when she woke a few hours later and discovered that her bag of money had not been stolen from her overnight.

Working is second nature to my mother. I was almost born en route to the hospital, as she had refused to take any time off work until she was actually in labor. One week after being released from the hospital, she was back at work again. The same thing happened with both my sister and brother.

And yet unlike my paternal grandmother, my mother has always been happy to let her spouse shine. She has always respected my father's leadership role and his way of life. She knows he is a man who likes to "bet his shirt" and has supported him all the way, using her soft power to smooth his harder edges.

She keeps everyone inside the company happy. She has displayed great love and sacrifice, even if that is not always obvious on the outside. She has been a great role model for me.

There are a number of other strong female leaders in Vietnam, as well. Most well known is Mai Kiều Liên, who turned state-owned dairy company Vinamilk into foreign portfolio investors' favorite company. In 2012, she became the first Vietnamese woman to enter the *Forbes* list of the fifty most powerful in Asia.

Then there is engineer Nguyễn Thị Mai Thanh, who worked her way up through the ranks to become chairwoman and CEO of home appliances, construction, and real estate company, REE Corp. In 2014, she entered the rankings of *Forbes Asia's* Fifty Power Businesswomen. The country also has a self-made female billionaire:

Nguyễn Thị Phương Thảo, who founded Vietnam's second-largest airline, VietJet Air.

Vietnam has several other female CEOs, and, overall, 73 percent of women are engaged in the workforce compared to 82 percent of men—according to the United Nations International Labour Organization (ILO). It is a very high percentage compared with other countries. There are many women working in factories, or who own small businesses, running their own shops and stalls.

But the ILO also says the high figure is misleading, since many women are in low-paying jobs. As a result, Vietnam only ranks 76 out of 108 countries in terms of female managers. The ILO undertook an analysis of job ads and discovered that 83 percent of managerial positions being advertised specified male-only candidates. When it came to director-level positions, the figure was 100 percent.

THP works hard to ensure we offer women the same opportunities as men. We have ten senior directors and four are women. My sister and I try to set a very strong example to the rest of the company; we work tirelessly to boost the number of female employees across it, as well.

It helps that our father has never discriminated between men and women. He just wants the right person for the job. He likes to use the analogy about a block of wood. It does not matter what kind of wood it is, because it can be carved according to need.

There are many departments at THP where women dominate, and many of them are customer-facing. We find that women are more consistent when it comes to the fine details and are less likely to defraud us. We also find that they are generally more loyal.

We would also really like to boost our female numbers in the sales department. Men are very good at closing deals, but they often seek to move on to the next kill. By contrast, women tend to care far more about providing good after-sales service, which is so important to THP.

However, we have found it difficult to recruit more women in this area, because it involves a lot of outdoor work, moving from stall to stall. The Vietnamese sun is very harsh—and pale skin is highly prized in Vietnam. For example, one of our best-known fairy tales, Tấm Cám, is a more violent version of Cinderella with some reincarnation thrown in. The evil stepsister dies after stepping into a bath of boiling water, thinking this is the secret to achieving pale skin and beauty.

I do not want to give the impression that women are somehow better than men. They are just different, and we seek to leverage those differences. But it is a battle to combat the structural sexism that exists in society.

Gender stereotypes and biases start very early. In 2017, the Ministry of Education and Training conducted a study with UNESCO. They examined seventy-six Vietnamese school textbooks and discovered that 95 percent of the important historical characters depicted were men.

Even worse, men were portrayed as doctors, scientists, and engineers, while women were shown as housewives, teachers, and office workers. Perhaps this is one of the reasons why I still detect a desire among some young women to marry a richer man and have an easy life.

The report's findings were not good, but conducting it was an important first step, and the ministry has pledged to rectify the situation. But women of my generation still struggle with routine sexism.

No one would dare to behave like this toward me at THP, but that is not the case when I step outside the office. Sometimes I attend meetings where a man will ask me if I will kiss him or even sleep with him. My general response is to just ignore what he is saying and focus on the official business agenda.

The worst example of sexual harassment occurred when I paid a courtesy call on a senior man in Hanoi. I would normally go with another colleague from the communications department. But that one time, he knew I was coming alone. He was about thirty years older than me, and when I stepped into his office, it was to the sight of him with his trousers down, exposing himself to me.

It was a shocking moment, and after momentarily freezing on the spot, I simply turned around and walked out. There was no point reporting it, because he was powerful. The next year when I paid the courtesy call again, I made sure I came with someone else and never mentioned the incident again. I hope he felt embarrassed or regretted his behavior—but somehow, I doubt it.

I had not dressed in a provocative manner. I like to dress well, and I want to be feminine—but I dress to succeed, not to seduce.

I normally try to make sure I bring someone else with me to a meeting. This makes it much harder for any men present to make even mildly suggestive comments. If that is not possible, then I often do one-on-ones with men I do not know well in a public venue. I always try my best to not give men an opening to go down an uncomfortable path. I often try to get to know their wives.

I also do not want to behave like a man, because I think there is great strength in a woman's negotiating skills and ability to listen. There is plenty of research demonstrating how a company's operational abilities improve when there are more women on the board.

But women need to make sure they stand up and be counted. It's best not to offer to make everyone else a cup of coffee until reaching a senior enough position where this is viewed as a positive gesture rather than a given.

Likewise, one of my friends told me she never offers to take notes in meetings. When her supervisor once asked her to, she said no. She turned it around and said, "In my experience, it's always women who are asked to take notes, and until we start refusing, it will stay that way. Do I have your support?"

> *Those five words—do I have your support?—are critical, because women cannot eliminate sexism on their own. We need men to help us dismantle it. The good news is that more and more men are eager to do this.*

Those five words—do I have your support?—are critical, because women cannot eliminate sexism on their own. We need men to help us dismantle it. The good news is that more and more men are eager to do this.

I have also reached my current position in life with my family at my side, but not a husband. At the turn of the century, it would have been unusual to find a woman in my position by the time she had reached her thirties. Increasingly, this is changing—but it is still quite rare. As a result, I am always getting asked when I will get married or if I have a boyfriend. But I have found ways to deflect the situation.

I simply tell them I am married—to THP.

ACKNOWLEDGMENTS

THE MORE SUBSTANTIAL A BOOK, the more substantial the debts an author must acknowledge. With gratitude, I wish to extend my heartfelt thanks to a number of people who have helped to make *Competing with Giants* what it is. Any success that *Competing with Giants* enjoys belongs to them.

To the extent that the book adds to—rather than subtracts from—the bewildering accounts of the ways multinational corporations operate in the globalized economy, the responsibility is entirely mine. To the extent that *Competing with Giants* is useful in describing the dynamics of how local companies can compete with and beat multinationals at their own game, I wish to acknowledge a number of individuals.

Nobody has been more important in the writing of this book than the members of the Trần family. I would like to thank my parents, whose love and guidance are with me in whatever I pursue. They are my ultimate role models, the ones who built THP into a playground where talented people could deploy their skills.

My appreciation goes first to my father, Trần Quí Thanh, whose vision and leadership of the Trần family and the company he founded has no limits. Every debt of gratitude that a daughter owes her father flows to a man whom history will record as a leader, and whose hard work, vision, and sacrifice created an organization which contributed to the prosperity of an entire nation. I appreciate my father for the wisdom that has found its way onto these pages.

With the same pride, I acknowledge the critical role played by my mother, Phạm Thị Nụ, who worked alongside my father to build THP into the successful organization it is today. The intelligence, energy, and boundless people skills of Madame Nu helped create the relationships and networks which enable the company to thrive. My mother's business acumen, grace, and support through every challenge continues to be an inspiration to me.

I thank my sister, Trần Ngọc Bích, and my brother, Trần Quốc Dũng, for their support while this book was being written and answering my relentless questions. The encouragement of my sister and brother was felt at every step of this journey and I am so appreciative.

I wish to thank my co-authors, Jackie Horne and John Kador. Jackie and John each contributed their experience and talents to make *Competing With Giants* a better book than I could have delivered myself. Jackie Horne, a long-standing business writer and editor, worked with me to bring THP's story to life and put it into its regional and historical context. As someone who spends part of the year in Asia and Europe, she has a firsthand view of how globalization is changing both regions and has earned my thanks for her participation during the many steps of this book's journey to publication.

John Kador, a talented business writer and wordsmith, worked with me to ensure that *Competing with Giants* would be accessible to leaders everywhere, as well as meaningful for business readers. A keen and enthusiastic observer of the globalized business world, John earned my great appreciation for his involvement in every aspect of preparing this book.

I am grateful to so many of my colleagues at THP for their willingness to be interviewed, answer questions and review parts of the manuscript. I especially thank the following people for their enthusiasm, expertise, and understanding: Peter Davies, Đoàn Việt Dũng, Lương Thị Duy Hiếu, Nguyễn Thu Trang, Nguyễn Hữu Thành, Nguyễn Kim Thoa, Nguyễn Văn Tư, Phạm Quang Chính, Roland Ruiz, Stefan Reicherstorfer, Tống Nhân Tôn, Trần Thanh Trấn Vũ, Vũ Phương Thanh, and Vương Thị Bích Liễu.

In addition, I express my heartfelt gratitude to a number of professionals who support the work of THP and generously offered my book the benefit of their wisdom and expertise. They are: Phạm Tấn Công, David Riddle, John Dawson, Richard Fitton, Diana Footitt, Terry Mahony, Nguyễn Tiến Vương, Kevin Snowball, Marshall Stocker, Terry Ting, Trịnh Hải Bằng, and Barry Weisblatt.

I am grateful to the professionals at Advantage|ForbesBooks for creating the very attractive package you are now holding. My gratitude goes to Keith Kopcsak, VP of Member Development; Saara Khalil, who served as a very capable account manager; Eland Mann, my editorial manager; Carly Blake, my cover designer; and Adam Vlach, my project manager.

Finally, I owe a great deal of gratitude to all the customers, partners, and vendors of THP. Without their loyalty, this book would not have been written. I beg forgiveness of all those who have been with me over the course of the years and whose names I have failed to mention. Together we embrace a tomorrow where local companies are better prepared to compete with giants. I give thanks to God for being my guide and directing me toward the light.

THP and Trần Family Timeline
(1953 to 2018)

1953

- Father Trần Quí Thanh born, Saigon

1957

- Mother Phạm Thị Nụ born, Saigon

1977

- Trần Quí Thanh joins the Ministry of Mechanics and Metallurgy; also starts a small yeast business

1979

- Trần Quí Thanh and Phạm Thị Nụ marry

1981

- Launches a sugar processing operation; expands into fructose in 1988

- Daughter Trần Uyên Phương born in Ho Chi Minh City

1984

- Daughter Trần Ngọc Bích born in Ho Chi Minh City

1986

- Son Trần Quốc Dũng born in Ho Chi Minh City

1994

- Launches the Ben Thanh Brewery-Beverage Factory, introduces flavored beer

- Establishes Tân Hiệp Phát to produce carbonated soft drinks

1995

- Launches Soya Milk in RGB (regular glass bottle) 250 milliliters

1996

- Launches Flash Beer

2000

- First beverage company in Vietnam to earn ISO 9002 certification from Det Norke Veritas (DNV)

2001

- Starts construction of factory and headquarters in Binh Duong Province.

- Launches Number 1 Energy Drink

- Completes successful advertising campaign for Number 1 Energy Drink

2002

- Number 1 Energy Drink is distributed across sixty provinces; honored as one of Southeast Asia's top ten beverage products

- Inaugurates Binh Duong plant and HQ

2003

- Announces goal to become Asia's leading company in the beverages, instant food, and packaging sector

- Launches Laser Beer

2004

- Implements a group re-structuring: upgrading infrastructure, production, and machinery

- Introduces Number 1 Soya Milk with advanced technology from Japan, becoming Vietnam's leading milk brand

- Begins bottling Number 1 Pure Water

2005

- Launches Bến Thành Gold Beer, leading in exploiting consumers' emotion in communication

2006

- Becomes the first in Vietnam to use PET bottles with the launch of Zero Degree Green Tea

- Packaging breakthrough allows THP to distribute Number 1 Soya Milk in paper packaging

- First Vietnam beverage company granted three integrated certificates: ISO 9001, ISO 14001, HACCP from DNV

- Launches: ED Carbonated Strawberry; Sport Drink Number 1 Active; Gold Draught Beer

2007

- Expands product range to include Number 1 Active; Number 1 Juicie Fruit; Number 1 Wintermelon Green Tea; Barley Zero Degree Tea

- Sponsors Vietnamese athletes to climb Mt. Everest with the motto, "Nothing is impossible"

2008:

- Launches Dr. Thanh Herbal Tea. Takes a record forty-five days of research and production using aseptic cold extraction technology to bring the product to market. Still holds a monopoly position in Vietnam

- Opens packaging plant

- Receives Vietnam Famous Brands award for two brands: Number 1 Energy Drink and Zero Degree Green Tea

2009

- Company reorganized to meet the challenge of becoming a $1 billion enterprise

- Launches VIP Café in PET bottle

2010

- Invests $2 million to deploy ERP (enterprise resource planning) system using SAP (systems, applications and products) software within five months and eight days

- Zero Degree Green Tea and Dr. Thanh Herbal Tea recognized as national brands under the Ministry of Industry and Trade's Vietnam Value program

- Receives merit from the prime minister of Vietnam in recognition of meritorious achievements in the cause of socialist construction and national defense

- Intellectual Property Association Vietnam names Trần Quí Thanh among Top 20 Entrepreneurs in Vietnam for outstanding achievements in brand construction and development

- Launches the carbonated green tea I-kun (lemon and strawberry)

2012

- Executes factory expansion project with the construction of the north's largest beverage factory, Number One Ha Nam

- Dr. Thanh receives the third-class Labor Medal presented by the president of Vietnam

- Zero Degree Green Tea, Dr. Thanh Herbal Tea, Number 1 Energy Drink accredited as national brands under the government's Vietnam Value campaign

- Groundbreaking for new factory at Chu Lai in Central Vietnam

2013

- Starts construction of Number 1 Hau Giang, the largest beverage plant in the southwest

- Kicks off project for distribution management software DMS Pro and applies PDA tools to support sales force

2014

- THP reaches one billion liters per year from an initial capacity of one million liters per year, an increase of one thousand times in twenty years

- Launches Zero Degree Oolong Tea

- Famous Brand awards for Dr. Thanh Herbal Tea, Zero Degree Green Tea, and Number 1 Energy Drink

2015

- Announces a new "Vision, Mission, and Core Values" for the years 2015 to 2035 to make THP a sustainable development organization

- Number One Ha Nam receives HACCP certification after one year in operation

- Awarded the prestigious award, Excellent Unit of the Association of Beer-Alcohol-Beverage for the community

2016

- *Financial Times* publishes special report about the life of "King of Vietnam Tea"

- Sponsors many social welfare programs including bridge building, water filters, breeding cows

- Builds internal control system for sales force and distributors

- Inaugurates Chu Lai plant and is recognized by Quang Nam People's Committee as construction marks the twentieth anniversary of Quan Nam Province

2017

- Launches book: *Dr. Thanh's Family Story*

- Dr. Thanh shares lessons about his successes and failures to a group of one thousand CEOs

- Launches website, tranquithanh.com, attracting many followers and readers

THP's Aspiration

Contribute to Vietnam's prosperity and make the country proud by creating a strong and sustainable national champion.

THP's Vision

Become Asia's leading food and beverage company.

THP's Mission

Produce high-quality and healthy products that comply with international standards and satisfy Asian consumer tastes. Meet our customers' current and future demands and be their preferred partner.

THP's Seven Core Values

1. Customer Satisfaction

- Take the initiative to listen, give detailed feedback, and meet the demands of customers, partners, suppliers, and related parties to achieve mutual goals and expectations in a timely fashion.

- Provide innovative and competitive product and service solutions, working for mutual benefit.

- Have a respectful and dedicated attitude toward all customers.

2. International Quality Standards

- Be committed to providing product and service quality to international standards.

- Implement advanced technological and management systems.

3. Responsible to the Community and Society

- Comply with environmental protection laws and food-safety regulations, implement the ISO 14000 and HACCP management systems.

- Make a positive impact on the community and wider society in all markets where THP does business.

- Make sustainable development a priority when choosing business partners.

4. Nothing Is Impossible

- Have a positive and can-do attitude. Always focus on results. Never give up until the desired results have been achieved.

- Dare to think differently, and approach problems with a willing spirit to conquer challenging goals.

- Connect and empower others to take action and pursue common goals. In case of failure, show colleagues how they can improve and learn from mistakes, turning a negative into a positive.

- Take responsibility and create opportunities for family members to maximize their capabilities. Always help others to realize the power of positivity, help them believe they can make positive changes in any situation, express confidence in coworkers.

5. Spirit of Business Ownership

- Believe that success and failure is thanks to your own efforts; do not blame external factors.

- Proactively make decisions, manage risk, and fulfill tasks within the scope of your responsibilities. Contribute to the team and achieve common goals.

- Understand your role and responsibilities within the team's achievements; above all, respect and protect the organization's interests, and make decisions beneficial to it.

- Confidently raise any issues hindering the group's achievements and goals, share information so colleagues can work better, whether you have been assigned to that job or not. Helping others achieve success becomes your success.

- Have an opinion and take actions to protect the company's image and branding, be proud of THP's staff and products.

6. Today Is Better Than Yesterday, But Not as Good as Tomorrow

- Constantly assess the present to develop innovative ideas for the future.

- Learn from success and failure, whether your own or that of others.

- Understand and encourage the spirit of learning, sharing, and innovative thinking.

- Strive to improve working methods, processes, and technologies to increase the efficiency and quality of THP's products and services.

7. Integrity

- Be respectful and committed; do the right thing at the right time; if you realize you cannot meet a commitment, inform the relevant person immediately, and handle the consequences with a positive mind-set, then keep moving forward.

- Stay positive and dedicated to the task at hand; do not repeat previous failures or feel ashamed of them; stay true to your word.

Trần Family Aspiration

Live life to the fullest; build boldly and create memorable achievements that are respected by the family and society.

Trần Family Mission

Share a culture of leadership, integrity, commitment, and talent so we can build a global business that creates wealth, enhances our family's reputation, and makes a positive impact on society.

Trần Family Core Values

1. Hard work means results, not possessions.

2. Contribute: Make a positive difference to others and think beyond self.

3. Integrity: Honor our word.

4. Maintain a "nothing is impossible" spirit.

5. Leadership: Being part of a family means taking responsibility to make things better for the family and live for its success.

BIBLIOGRAPHY

An, Hoai. "Retail Revenue to Reach $179 Billion by 2020." *Vietnam Economic Times*. May 18, 2016. http://vneconomictimes.com/article/vietnam-today/retail-revenue-to-reach-179-billion-by-2020.

Asian Development Bank. "Poverty in Vietnam." 2017. https://www.adb.org/countries/viet-nam/poverty.

Bhattacharya, Rina. *Inflation Dynamics and Monetary Policy Transmission in Vietnam and Emerging Asia*. International Monetary Fund Working Papers. July 3, 2013. https://www.imf.org/external/pubs/ft/wp/2013/wp13155.pdf.

Bin, Chua Hak, and Lee Ju Yee. *Vietnam Rising*. Maybank Kim Eng. August 2017.

Brand Finance. *Nation Brands 2016: The Annual Report on the World's Most Valuable Nation Brands*. October 2016.

Cecco, Leyland, and Annie Sakkab. "Vietnamese Refugee Turns Flight into Art in Canada." The United Nations High Commissioner for Refugees. July 1, 2017. http://www.unhcr.org/uk/news/stories/2017/7/5953acb04/vietnamese-refugee-turns-flight-art-canada.html.

Central Intelligence Agency. "The World Factbook—East and Southeast Asia: Vietnam." May 1, 2018. https://www.cia.gov/library/Publications/the-world-factbook/geos/vm.html.

Central Intelligence Agency. "The World Factbook—Field Listing: Urbanization." Accessed 2018. https://www.cia.gov/library/publications/the-world-factbook/fields/2212.html.

Chi, Khanh. "Banned Coca-Cola Drinks Now Certified." *Vietnam Economic Times.* May 7, 2016. http://vneconomictimes.com/article/business/banned-coca-cola-drinks-now-certified.

Coca-Cola. "Coca-Cola Announces US $300 Million Investment for Strong and Sustainable Growth in Vietnam." Press Release. October 26, 2012. https://www.coca-colacompany.com/press-center/press-releases/coca-cola-announces-us-300-million-investment-for-strong-and-sustainable-growth-in-vietnam.

Davies, Nick. "Vietnam Forty Years On: How a Communist Victory Gave Way to Capitalist Corruption." April 22, 2010. https://www.theguardian.com/news/2015/apr/22/vietnam-40-years-on-how-communist-victory-gave-way-to-capitalist-corruption.

Encyclopedia of the New American Nation. "The Vietnam War and Its Impact—Refugees and "Boat People." Accessed 2018. http://www.americanforeign-relations.com/O-W/The-Vietnam-War-and-Its-Impact-Refugees-and-boat-people.html.

Facts and Details. "Vietnam After the Vietnam War." factsanddetails.com. Accessed 2018. http://factsanddetails.com/southeast-asia/Vietnam/sub5_9a/entry-3369.html.

Facts and Details. "Vietnam's Stock Exchange and Banks." factsanddetails.com. Accessed 2018. http://factsanddetails.com/southeast-asia/Vietnam/sub5_9g/entry-3476.html.

Forbes Asia. "Asia's 50 Power Businesswomen: Mai Kieu Lien." Forbes.com. February 29, 2012. https://www.forbes.com/lists/2012/13/power-women-asia-12_Mai-Kieu-Lien_KI0V.html.

Forbes Asia. "Asia's 50 Power Businesswomen: Nguyễn Thị Phương Thảo." Forbes.com. 2014. https://www.forbes.com/pictures/fdgk45ggee/nguyen-thai-mai-thanh-61-vietnam/#1e5c31a528e3.

Forbes Corporate Communications. "*Forbes* Releases Seveneth Annual World's Most Valuable Brands List." *Forbes.* May 23, 2017. https://www.forbes.com/

sites/forbespr/2017/05/23/forbes-releases-seventh-annual-worlds-most-valu-able-brands-list/#f446e975b55d.

Horne, Jackie. "Vietnam's Private Sector Ventures Offshore." FinanceAsia. November 3, 2017. https://www.financeasia.com/News/440667,vietnams-private-sector-ventures-offshore.aspx.

Horne, Jackie. "Vietnam Tries to Speed Up Privatisation Programme." FinanceAsia. November 6, 2017. https://www.financeasia.com/News/440668,vietnam-tries-to-speed-up-privatisation-programme.aspx.

International Labour Organization. "More Women in Management is Good for Business." Press Release. January 12, 2015. http://www.ilo.org/hanoi/Informationresources/Publicinformation/Pressreleases/WCMS_336061/lang--en/index.htm.

International Labour Organization. "Public Information: Vietnam." Accessed 2018. http://www.ilo.org/hanoi/Informationresources/Publicinformation/lang--en/index.htm.

Isaacs, Arnold R. *Vietnam Shadows: The War, Its Ghosts, and Its Legacy.* John Hopkins University Press. March 2000.

Kornai, János, and Yingyi Qian, eds. *Market and Socialism: In the Light of the Experiences of China and Vietnam.* Palgrave Macmillan. November 2008.

Leinster, Colin. "Vietnam Business Rushes to Get In the Country Could be Poised for Stunning Economic Growth. While the US Government Keeps America Out, Japanese and Europeans are Investing Heavily." *FORTUNE Magazine.* April 5, 1993. http://archive.fortune.com/magazines/fortune/fortune_archive/1993/04/05/77692/index.htm.

Mishel, Lawrence, and Jessica Schieder. "CEOs Make 276 Times More than Typical Workers." Economic Policy Institute. August 3, 2016. https://www.epi.org/publication/ceos-make-276-times-more-than-typical-workers/.

Mexico National Institute of Public Health. "Why it is Not Possible to Make Determinations on the Usefulness of the Tax on Sugar Sweetened Beverages in Mexico During 2015 Using Raw Sales Data." Gob.mx. 2017. https://www.insp.mx/epppo/blog/4063-tax-sugar-sweetened-beverages.html.

Moore, Malcom. "'Mass Suicide' Protest at Apple Manufacturer Foxconn Factory." *The Telegraph*. January 11, 2012. https://www.telegraph.co.uk/news/worldnews/asia/china/9006988/Mass-suicide-protest-at-Apple-manufacturer-Foxconn-factory.html.

Nhung, Hong. "Vietnam Again Fifth in Consumer Confidence in Q3 2017." *Vietnam Economic Times*. November 11, 2018. http://www.vneconomictimes.com/article/vietnam-today/vietnam-again-fifth-in-consumer-confidence-in-q3-2017.

Nielsen. *Made in … which Country? Global Brand Origin Report*. April 2016. Published April 2016.

Perkins, Dwight H., and Vu Thanh Tu Anh. *Vietnam's Industrial Policy: Designing Policies for Sustainable Development*. Harvard Kennedy School Ash Institute for Democratic Governance and Innovation. Harvard Policy Dialogue Papers. 2007.

Poushter, Jacob. "Worldwide, People divided on Whether Life is Better than in the Past." Pew Research Centre. December 5, 2017. http://www.pewglobal.org/2017/12/05/worldwide-people-divided-on-whether-life-today-is-better-than-in-the-past/.

PXP Vietnam Asset Management. *Vietnam Smaller Companies Fund*. July 2017.

S&P Global Market Intelligence.

Statista. "Principal Rice Exporting Countries Worldwide in 2017 / 2018 (in 1,000 metric tons)." February 2018. https://www.statista.com/statistics/255947/top-rice-exporting-countries-worldwide-2011/.

Statista. "Soft Drinks: Vietnam." 2018. https://www.statista.com/outlook/20020000/127/soft-drinks/vietnam#market-revenue.

Statista. "The Coca-Cola Company's Net Operating Revenues Worldwide from 2007 to 2017 (in Billion US dollars)." 2018. https://www.statista.com/statistics/233371/net-operating-revenues-of-the-coca-cola-company-worldwide/.

Tam, Duong. "Sexist School Textbooks Holding Back Gender Equality in Vietnam: Report." Vietnam Express International. August 29, 2017. https://e.vnexpress.net/news/news/sexist-school-textbooks-holding-back-gender-equality-in-vietnam-report-3634277.html.

Thao, Phoung. "VN Index Beats the One-Thousand-Point Level." *The Saigon Times*. January 4, 2018. http://english.thesaigontimes.vn/57854/VN-Index-beats-the-1000-point-level.html.

The World Bank. "Exports of Goods and Services (% of GDP)." 2016. https://data.worldbank.org/indicator/NE.EXP.GNFS.ZS.

The World Bank. "GDP World Growth (Annual %)." 2016. https://data.worldbank.org/indicator/NY.GDP.MKTP.KD.ZG?locations=VN.

The World Bank. "Vietnam." Accessed 2018. https://data.worldbank.org/country/vietnam.

Transparency International. *Corruptions Perception Index 2016*. January 25, 2017. https://www.transparency.org/news/feature/corruption_perceptions_index_2016.

Transparency International. *Corruptions Perception Index 2017*. February 21, 2018. https://transparency.am/en/cpi.

UNESCO Institute for Statistics, the UNESCO International Institute for Educational Planning, and the International Institute for Educational Planning Pôle de Dakar. *Who Pays for What in Education: The Real Costs Revealed through National Education Accounts*. UNESCO. 2016.

University of Pennsylvania Warthon. "Coca-Cola's Failed Bid for China Huiyuan Juice: The Return of Protectionism?" Knowledge @ Wharton. April 1, 2009. http://knowledge.wharton.upenn.edu/article/coca-colas-failed-bid-for-china-huiyuan-juice-the-return-of-protectionism/.

Vietnam Chamber of Commerce and Industry. *VCCI Annual Report 2007*. June 2008.

Vietnam Investment Review. "Binh Duong Surpasses Annual FDI Target in Nine Months." October 2, 2017. http://www.vir.com.vn/binh-duong-surpasses-annual-fdi-target-in-nine-months-52642.html.

Vietnam Ministry of Finance. "Stock Market Outlook in the Second Half of 2009." July 30, 2009. https://bit.ly/2L0A83M.

Vietnamnet Bridge. "Millennial Shoppers to Drive Future of Vietnam's E-Commerce Market." November 14, 2017. http://english.vietnamnet.vn/fms/

business/190228/millennial-shoppers-to-drive-future-of-vietnam-s-e-commerce-market.html.

Vietnamnet Bridge. "Vietnam's GDP Per Capita Tops $2,200." December 29, 2016. http://english.vietnamnet.vn/fms/business/170401/vietnam-s-gdp-per-capita-tops--2-200.html.

White, Spencer, Stephen Corry, Willie Chan, and Alistair Scarff. *Asain Insights*. Merrill Lynch. February 2, 2006.

Worldometers. "Vietnam Population (Live)." Accessed 2018. http://www.worldometers.info/world-population/vietnam-population/.

Zucman, Gabriel. "The Desperate Inequality Behind Global Tax Dodging." *The Guardian*. November 8, 2017. https://www.theguardian.com/commentisfree/2017/nov/08/tax-havens-dodging-theft-multinationals-avoiding-tax.

Phương Uyên Trần is currently Deputy CEO of the THP Group, Vietnam's leading beverage company. In addition to running Number 1 Chu Lai, she is also responsible for THP's overall procurement, domestic and international marketing, public relations, and corporate social responsibility programs.

Phương is an executive of the Beverage Association of Vietnam. She also sits on the executive committee of the Young Presidents' Organization (YPO) Vietnam chapter where she ranks as the youngest woman to have been accepted globally when she joined in 2007. She is passionate about how family-owned businesses are built and sustained, training in the subject at Harvard University in the US, the International Institute for Management Development (IMD) in Switzerland, and with YPO.

In 2017, she organized a family business workshop for over five hundred business owners alongside *Business Magazine* in Vietnam, one of the first of its kind in the country. She is keen to share her knowledge and regularly speaks about the challenges and opportunities of managing family-owned businesses at conferences around the world. Phương lives in Ho Chi Minh City, Vietnam.

Jackie Horne is a business journalist, editor, and author who divides her time between the UK, Hong Kong, and Sri Lanka. After graduating from Cambridge University with a master's degree in history, she went on to work for the BBC, as well as co-own and edit Asian business publisher FinanceAsia.com. She is also a director of the Schools Relief Initiative, an educational and environmental NGO based in Sri Lanka.

John Kador is the author of more than twenty business books on leadership, entrepreneurship, finance, and business ethics. He graduated from Duke University with a degree in English and earned a master's of public relations degree from The American University. He lives with his wife, a retired psychologist, in Pennsylvania, USA.

OUR SERVICES

The Tân Hiệp Phát Beverage Group (THP) is Vietnam's leading privately held FMCG (fast-moving consumer goods) company. The family-owned business was founded by Trần Quí Thanh (Dr. Thanh) in 1994 and is known throughout Asia for its innovative consumer products.

At THP we develop, produce, and distribute three of Vietnam's most popular national brands and supply beverages and other products throughout Vietnam and sixteen countries worldwide. Our products include herbal teas, green teas, sports drinks, energy drinks, soya milk, and purified water.

From humble roots making yeast and then sugar, THP has rapidly evolved into a company focused on creating healthy and preservative-free beverages using the most advanced bottling equipment in the world. The business continues to be owned and managed by the Tran family, who is committed to building an increasingly international business with roots and values grounded firmly in Vietnamese culture.

THP employs over five thousand people across its four production facilities and dozens of branch offices. We make ongoing investments into researching new ways to better serve our consumers. Our factories are home to state-of-the-art technologies including ten aseptic lines, PET manufacturing systems, and both hot and cold filling lines for Tetra Pak, cans and glass bottles. We also produce our own packaging including PET and cartons. We are passionate about our products and continuously strive to create new and exciting consumer brands. Our headquarters is located in Binh Duong, a suburb of Ho Chi Minh City in southern Vietnam.

We believe it is critical for every company steward to make a lasting contribution to the community, particularly toward young people, so that the next generation has as many opportunities as possible. To that end, we heavily invest in supporting social activities throughout the nation. These corporate social responsibility activities include: building bridges for local communities, supporting athletic opportunities for young people, and sharing Vietnamese art and culture with the world.

We hope that this book inspires and empowers entrepreneurs everywhere to pursue their dreams. There is no limit to what individuals who are willing to work hard and are blessed with a little luck can achieve. THP's story is a testament to one man's vision. The fact that millions of consumers around the world are loyally drinking THP beverages every day is also testament to the execution of that vision by a team of highly motivated individuals.

We invite readers to sample a THP beverage (www.thp.com.vn) and, as we raise our glasses, to drink to a future together as we continue to invest in and create a better world for the next generation with passion, creativity, and energy. Please start a conversation with us by emailing info@thp.com.vn, calling +84 8 987 60066, or sending a letter to 219 Highway Binh Duong, Vinh Phu Commune, Thuan An Town, Binh Duong, 72000, Vietnam.

We also invite you to get in touch if you would like coaching or consultancy services to help compete with giants. Please email us at info@competingwithgiants.vn.

A Special Offer from ForbesBooks

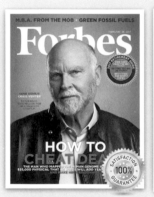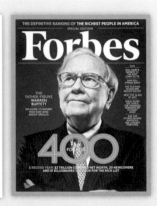

Other publications bring you business news. Subscribing to *Forbes* magazine brings you business knowledge and inspiration you can use to make your mark.

- Insights into important business, financial and social trends
- Profiles of companies and people transforming the business world
- Analysis of game-changing sectors like energy, technology and health care
- Strategies of high-performing entrepreneurs

Your future is in our pages.

To see your discount and subscribe go to Forbesmagazine.com/bookoffer.

Forbes